Ditch THE PEOPLE PLEASER

A *Radical* GUIDE TO NOT BEING NICE

By Kara V Grant

Copyright © 2020 Kara V Grant

www.soulconfidence.co.uk

A catalogue record for this book is available from the British Library.

ISBN: 978-1-9162504-9-9

Although the author and publisher have made every effort to ensure that the information in this book was correct at press time, the author and publisher do not assume and hereby disclaim any liability to any party for any loss, damage, or disruption caused by errors or omissions, whether such errors or omissions result from negligence, accident, or any other cause. This book is not intended as a substitute for the medical advice of physicians. The reader should regularly consult a physician in matters relating to his/her health and particularly with respect to any symptoms that may require diagnosis or medical attention.

Cover and interior design by Michelle Catanach
www.michellecatanach.co.uk

To Arthur and Archie. For reminding me why I ditched the people pleaser. With all my love x

I picked up the scattered pieces of myself,
Where I had discarded me throughout the years.
I pulled her in and pulled her close,
And told her with love, 'Now tell me your fears.'

~ Kara V Grant

A Message From Kara

I wrote my first book aged 10 years old.

I filled up those small, lined yellow notebooks with pages and pages of writing, spilling my innermost thoughts (and sometimes turmoil) out onto the paper, the pen a vessel for my inner voice. In some hormonal teenage rage I threw them out, adamant no one would ever read my childish musings. How I would love to read those books now! Following that, writing became limited to course work and something I endured, rather than enjoyed. It wasn't until I started journaling several years later that I realised how much I could express myself freely – especially those untapped parts – through writing.

Having read (and been inspired by) hundreds of non-fiction books - some good, some bad, and others sublime – a seed began to grow. Was I brave enough to write about my stories and experiences and put myself and all my vulnerabilities out into the world? Was it possible that, by sharing my own experiences and insights, I could help others on their journey of transformation and healing? The arrival of social media and its various platforms as tools for self-expression gave me a glimmer of possibility. So, I dived in – and this book is the result.

I talk a lot about women in this book. That doesn't mean that if you're not a woman it isn't for you. If you picked up this book, resonated with the title and wanted to learn more, then this is absolutely for you. People pleasing isn't reserved for women; I have worked with many men who've put other people first, who people please, and who want to be 'nice'. I hope that, whether you are male, female or non-binary, you find the support you need in this book to ditch your need to please.

I'm very aware that I'm writing from a privileged position of being a white, heterosexual, cis gendered, able-bodied woman, and what I share is reflective of that. Writing this book has opened my eyes further to how different my life and experiences may have been without these privileges and the head start in life they afforded me. People pleasing is something that can affect us all. My desire is that this book gives you what you need.

Throughout this book, you're going to hear personal anecdotes from friends and clients (shared with their permission). Their honesty and willingness to share some of their experiences humbled me. Thank you to each of you who contributed.

As I write this book, the world is in turmoil; a constant state of uncertainty abounds. Current affairs appear rooted in white supremacy – white police killing Black people; climate change; the huge disparity between the top 1% and the amount of people living in poverty; right wing politics and inflammatory rhetoric; institutionalised racism; war; floods; bush fires ... not to mention a global pandemic that has wiped economies and exacerbated poverty and abuse (as if they needed to get any worse!).

Fear, hatred and prejudice are being seen in the cold light of day, no longer hidden in the shadows. The binary thinking of the majority is creating more division and conflict while personal identities are being shattered, causing people to question their place in the world the more the veil lifts. As a sensitive, you feel it all. Your world isn't fixed or binary. You see all the complexities and nuances and, despite the heaviness you sometimes feel in your heart, you know that you can use your sensitive gifts to create a more peaceful, kinder, fairer and equitable world.

What do you feel will help to contribute to change? People pleasing, trying to be 'nice' and keeping yourself small? Or, embracing all of who you are, knowing and expressing your needs, and being compassionate and empathetic without burnout or resentment? In short, do you want to show up fully in - and for - life? If you do then your people pleaser needs to step aside so you can pave the way.

If you're asking yourself 'how' right now, there's a reason you picked up this book! *Ditch the People Pleaser* will take you on a journey of self-exploration and discovery so that you can learn to embrace your sensitive gifts and use them to effect positive change in all areas of your life, without your inner people pleaser holding you back. In each chapter I give you time to reflect, and suggest aligned actions you can take as well as resources you can use. As in all of my work, I talk about what you can do for your mind, body, breath and spirit so that you can be present to all the joy in your life.

Before you go any further, I'd like you to first ask yourself: Why?

Why do you need to quit people pleasing? Why do you want to stop being 'nice' and instead start to embrace being *all* of you? Whenever you feel that you want to retreat or the work feels too heavy, come back to your why; it will keep pointing you to where your heart desires you to go.

I would love for you to embark on this book with an open heart and mind and 100% committed to doing the work. I suggest you take the time to use the resources and reflection points, to dig deep AND take the action.

And please join my free Facebook community **The Sensitive Superstars Movement** for support from other sensitive people who get what it means to be a people pleaser. You are not alone, no matter how lonely doing the deeper work may feel at times. But remember: only *you* can do the work to be the change.

Contents

Introduction

Imagine this: You are a little girl watching your favourite Disney movie where the 'good' girl always wins. She does as she is told, tolerates harmful and abusive behaviours, is overly polite, painfully shy, and dreams of being rescued by a handsome Prince. Which she is. Repeatedly. She obligingly accepts his hand in marriage - because that is what good and oh-so-deserving girls do - and they live happily ever after (a life undoubtedly riddled with co-dependency, not that we see that part). And so the narrative goes, movie after movie after movie.

Snow White, Belle and Ariel all taught us that to be loved you need to shut up, tolerate (at the expense of your own happiness and desires), and put your needs last. Anything else would be selfish, unacceptable, and unworthy of admiration, respect, and that ever-desired self-worth-measuring promise of marriage!

We have grown up in a culture that encourages you to be nice, to please, and to put others and their feelings before your own (even when you feel unsafe, and your intuition is screaming alarm bells at you). One of the earliest things I repeatedly heard was 'be a good girl' aka play nicely, share, be quiet, and do not complain. Snow White, Belle and Ariel - to name only a few Disney characters - were all, you guessed it, nice. The underlying implication is that being nice = being accepted = getting the dress/the shoe/the partner and the happy ever after.

When I asked on social media, 'What stories/ nursery rhymes/ Disney films do you remember reading or watching that told you what being a nice girl was like?' all the responses referenced the put-upon female Disney characters. Cinderella, in particular, was noted as being a female victim who puts up with bullying and abuse until a man rescues her and 'makes her happy'.

After Disney, I grew up watching music videos and reading magazines such as More, Cosmo and Heat, where women could be praised one week and vilified the next, simply for what she wore, or for gaining (or losing) a few pounds. In my late teens/early twenties, the internet and social media became gospel, and images and words of what a 'nice' girl was, how to keep a man happy, what attractive looked like, and the drip-feeding of shaming assertive women was furthermore burned into my brain. Videos, pictures, words – implicitly, explicitly, and sometimes subliminally – became my frame of reference for what was 'normal' and acceptable.

In the media, mainstream pop and films demonstrate women putting others needs before their own as good: the girl next door - nice, sweet and helpful - versus the selfish, assertive and 'brazen' one.

Madonna is a prime example of this. She is, in many ways, a trailblazer, always pushing boundaries and challenging the status quo. Always expressing herself in the ways that she wants to, not according to gender stereotypes and what is 'acceptable' as a woman. She pleases herself, not others. The media, naturally, love to hate on her. Each decade has brought a new level of criticism - her relationships, marriage, parenting, body, age. We would struggle to find a white, cis-man who has been under such scrutiny.

We do not need to travel too far back in time to see this is a story that has played out for centuries. Let's face it, men have generally written history. The history books are dominated by men who have long since rejected, felt threatened by, and shown abhorrence for women who challenge the status quo.

Burning 'witches' at the stake is the perfect example of this. These were the kinds of men who preferred women to be quiet, submissive, dutiful and to conform; otherwise, she would be justifiably punished. Remember, domestic violence and spousal rape were legal and socially acceptable until relatively recently in parts of the Western world. And, even though attitudes and laws have changed, it still happens. Shockingly, given that we are in 2020, there is no legislation or protection for women in many countries across the world. A study by World Bank in Feb 2018 ('Global and Regional Trends in Women's Legal Protection Against Domestic Violence and Sexual Harassment') found that close to 1.4 billion women lack legal protection against domestic economic violence.

Side note: this is not an 'anti-men' rant. This is not #allmen. I get that. I know many men who love and respect women. However, the ones who did not, the ones who wrote the history books, the ones who upheld - and continue to defend - the Patriarchy are those I am describing.

Carol Gilligan defines it this way: 'Patriarchy is a culture based on a gender binary and hierarchy, a framework or lens that leads us to see human capacities as either 'masculine' (e.g. independence, rationality, emotional stoicism, the mind) or 'feminine' (dependence, emotional sensitivity, caregiving, the body) and to privilege the masculine. It elevates some men over other men and all men over women.' Don't get me wrong, women are not absolved of responsibility here. Many of us carry internalised misogyny, thus upholding the status quo, more of which I will discuss in chapter 11. But people pleasing is so deeply entrenched in our collective psyche. It is time to start examining why and take a radically honest look at the ways we - as individuals - have maintained the status quo.

In this book, we are going to explore four of the areas where you may find yourself people pleasing: life, relationships (including love and sex), work, and business and leadership. I will share real life stories and experiences, some personal and some from people who have wanted to contribute their anecdotes to this book. I will ask you to draw parallels in these stories and identify how, where and why you people please. This is not a passive experience. I want you to be engaged and taking aligned action throughout.

Alongside my experiences, research and others' stories, I have included reflection points to give you the opportunity to pause, breathe, and to check in with you and your inner people pleaser. I have also included the 7-Step Exploration at the back of the book (section five), an incremental process that will help you further explore and dismantle people pleasing. For the reflections and 7-Step Exploration, I would highly recommend treating yourself to a new journal (any excuse!!), and meditating (or doing some other meditative activity) beforehand. The resources I give you come from practices and techniques I have used myself and with the people I've worked with. Not everything will resonate and not everything will be for you. Take what you need.

Eradicating people pleasing from the world is part of my mission. Yes, it feels daunting at times, but I am all about taking one step after the other and changing the world one people-pleaser at a time. I have been there. I have waded in the treacle. I have walked in the fire (and every other personal development analogy you can think of). I have lived to tell the tale so that now I can support you on your journey. So, let us start exploring ...

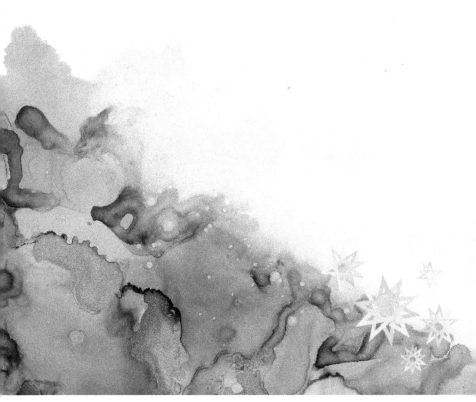

Section 1

People Pleasing ... In Life

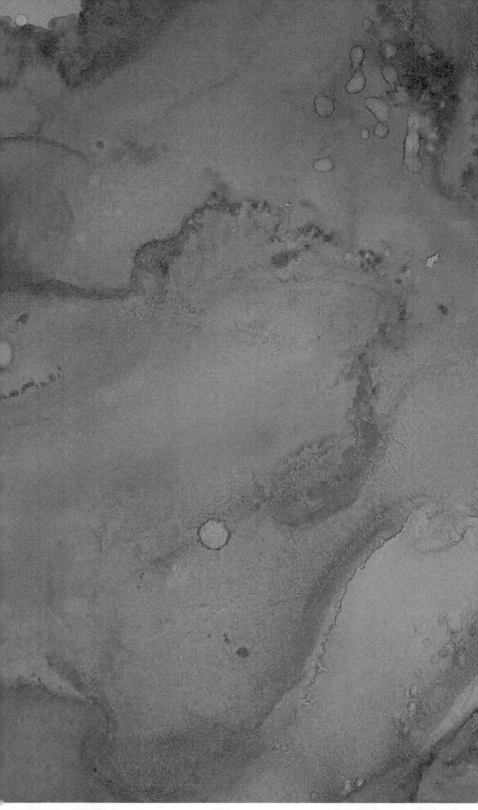

People pleasing is a social and personal construct designed to maintain the status quo (from the micro to the macro). It disempowers and causes us to disengage from true compassion, suffocating creativity and courage. In life it creates resentment, burnout and overwhelm. When you start to unpack your people pleaser you begin to see things more clearly.

In this section, we are going to dive deep into the societal and cultural stories and experiences that enable people pleasing to be so dominant. We will begin to deconstruct your conditioning, equipping you with some fantastic practical tools and techniques that can set you on the path to ditching your people pleaser.

You will discover where your people pleasing story started, knowing this is not about blame or shame. It's not about blaming someone else for passing it on to you, or about shaming yourself for having a people pleaser. It is about taking full responsibility for where you are right now while being deeply compassionate to yourself. We will touch on some of the science behind people pleasing and on the impact people pleasing can have at all levels. It is also crucial that you get clear on the legacy you want to leave behind for the next generation; the impact of continued people pleasing on younger people around you and how to break the cycle.

1
Craving Approval

L et's talk about THAT person. You know the one – the popular guy/girl at school, the super sharp stylish mamma you have met at a baby group, the cool AF online influencer you follow. THAT person. You want them to like you so much. Because somehow being liked by the 'cool kid' validates your very existence.

I don't want to think about how much of my energy, creativity and ingenuity I used up trying to please that person at different points in my life. From what I wore around them to constructing something witty to say – I craved their approval so much. In my mind, they were clearly so much better than me; if they liked me then somehow I would be a better person. This is something that is relatively easy to let go of as you start ditching your people pleaser. As you value yourself more you begin to like yourself more. When you like and appreciate yourself, the need to impress people you don't know starts to diminish. Remember, you have all the tools throughout this book to support your personal journey.

In real life and on social media, there are layers and layers of this people-pleasing thing. I've been caught up in what I was posting on social media because I wanted the people who I follow - the cool kids - to approve of what I was writing.

I wanted validation from people whose opinions matter to me. When I realised that I was doing this, I checked myself. While I can admire these people, their returning the admiration doesn't actually make a difference to me and my value in the world.

There is an episode of *Black Mirror* called *Nosedive*. In it, the protagonist is so desperate for ratings on social media that her life goes from super sanitised pastel-coloured perfection to a grubby mess. Why? Because she didn't get the approval that she so desperately sought which took its toll. While social media has brought about many benefits, we cannot deny the psychosocial impact of such platforms and the need for 'likes' and validation.

Social media can amplify your people pleaser.

When we look at how important our formative relationships are, it makes sense that we crave approval from others. If we're not accepted, then by default we're rejected, which goes against our survival instincts. Early stories about what being selfish is and how you need to be nice don't disappear when you become an adult. But, as adults, our validation can no longer be sustained via other peoples' approval. We are no longer dependent on others – or their approval of us – to survive. Our survival instincts, however, didn't get this memo – they are still triggered by rejection. External validation is fleeting and temporary. Self-compassion and self-respect are permanent and are what is needed to shift towards self-acceptance.

When I first started talking about people pleasing it was really interesting to hear and read some of the comments. I heard from some people saying that they did not want to be selfish by putting themselves first. Some were indignant, insisting they *had* to people please, like there was no other option and this was what made you a 'good' human. This belief is deeply ingrained.

So, let us look at the biological/evolutionary need to be accepted and what you need to feel safe and loved. Thousands of years ago, when we lived in smaller 'tribal' communities, rejection from the family group would have led to death – either by hungry sabre-toothed tigers, or other clans. Our primitive ('reptilian') brain controlled our automatic self-preserving behaviours to ensure our survival. Anything that was a threat to our safety (survival) would have stimulated our amygdala and alerted our sympathetic nervous system, flooding our body with adrenaline and cortisol and triggering the fight-flight-freeze response; this was enough to stop us doing anything that risked rejection from the community.

We have evolved in how we live our lives but we still have our primitive brain. Our environment may have changed and we may not be faced with the same threats as our ancestors, but we are still met with potentially dangerous situations. When we feel threatened (or *perceive* that we are under threat), the same survival response is triggered. Someone not accepting you can stimulate your amygdala, which sends a message to your sympathetic nervous system, and thus the same internal response is created. It's this response that we then become reactive to, manifesting as seemingly irrational or destructive behaviours. Understanding this is vital to understanding why certain situations trigger you.

Maslow's Hierarchy of Needs

You might be familiar with Maslow's hierarchy of needs which state the order of human needs:

1. Physiological

2. Safety

3. Belonging and Love

4. Esteem

5. Self-Actualization

'Physiological' and 'safety' are your most basic needs for survival and comprise food and shelter (and, in a capitalist society, the money to pay for them). Belonging, love and esteem are classed as your emotional needs, and self-actualisation is considered your self-fulfilment (growth) need. Generally, people must meet lower level needs before moving on to the next level. If someone is living hand-to-mouth each month and struggling to meet the most basic needs of food and shelter, then love and belonging might not be a priority.

People pleasing can impact our needs being met and where we sit according to Maslow's hierarchy. When we seek approval and prioritise meeting the needs of others (at the expense of our own), we remain stuck at the bottom of the hierarchy. This can look like tolerating hurtful and abusive behaviours and not 'rocking the boat' to ensure our needs for safety are met. When we seek love and belonging, we may people please to ensure that those needs are met, believing that pleasing others is the only way to feel loved and gain a sense of belonging. It's easy to see how, when we are stuck in a cycle of people-pleasing, our self-actualisation (growth) is restricted, or seemingly unattainable.

On the flipside, when we prioritise (and take responsibility for) our own needs over others, and learn to esteem ourselves from the inside (instead of relying on external validation), we can see how growth becomes possible. Now, this isn't to say that once you reach self-actualisation you'll never drop back to the bottom of the hierarchy (physiological and safety) – such is the paradox that we can be growing AND find ourselves living in survival mode. We've certainly seen this with the global pandemic as people lost their jobs and income and had to re-prioritise their most basic of needs. However, we can clearly see how people-pleasing stunts our growth and stops us from reaching our full potential in all aspects of our lives.

Before I go on I want to make a clear distinction between people-pleasing and cooperation, and this is particularly important to understand if you have (or work with) children. I've often heard people praise children who want to please others as though it's a really positive thing. Let me tell you now: it's not. We do *not* want to raise people pleasers. So many of us are experiencing psychological issues as adults *because of* people pleasing as children.

Of course, we want our children to cooperate and to be kind. Firstly, there is a huge difference between being 'nice' and being kind. Niceness comes from the head (ego); kindness comes from the heart. If you've ever experienced any kind of emotional abuse, you'll know that the most abusive and narcissistic of people (I'm talking traits, not disorder here) can also be the most charming to the outside world. Equally, as people pleasers, our need to be nice comes from our egoic need for approval.

Cooperation, and learning to get along in a society with other humans, is a survival strategy (as discussed earlier). This learning occurs as a natural part of the socialisation process (albeit much socialisation nowadays is forced and occurs in very artificial environments, e.g. many mainstream schools). And while cooperation sounds very similar to people pleasing, it's really about being an equal member of society. It's about ensuring *everyone's* needs are met. Egalitarian societies - for example, hunter-gatherer communities - require cooperation because everyone is equal and all resources are shared equally. People pleasing, however, follows a different dynamic. It's about power and control, the people pleaser essentially taking the role of the 'victim' or, more typically, the 'martyr'. For people pleasing to work as a dynamic, there has to be a person assuming control and taking the 'perpetrator' role; there are no equals.

So, as parents (or anyone who works with children in any capacity), when we approve of our child's 'need to please' what we're really saying is this: I approve of you behaving in a way that makes me more comfortable and is more palatable to me and other adults. And, if we want to go a step further, we're saying: you make me look like a better parent (teacher/care worker etc.) i.e. you make me look like I'm in control (hidden inference: of myself). As most of us do not live in egalitarian societies, it's fair to assume that children are generally viewed as 'lesser than' and therefore expected to perform in a way that is acceptable (and convenient) to adults.

As a child, if your needs were not met by those you depended on to meet them, you will likely have made it your responsibility to meet theirs. People pleasing would have been a survival instinct. If you identify as being a people pleaser as a child, then it's likely that your basic needs were not met. Going back to Maslow's hierarchy of needs, even if you were fed, clothed and had a roof over your head, you may not have moved beyond your physiological needs (level 1). The need to feel safe (level 2) requires emotional and spiritual safety, not just physical. While many of our parents and ancestors could provide for our physical safety, if they were stuck in survival mode and themselves not feeling emotionally safe (or suppressed their emotions), they would not have been able to provide that level of safety for us.

Many of us were raised by emotionally unhealthy adults who projected their trauma and wounds, or were emotionally unavailable; cyclical patterns that repeat each generation when left unchecked. This would have exacerbated our need to please those around us, bonding us to their pain and creating co-dependent parent-child relationships. Luckily, we have much more awareness of emotional health and neuroscience now, and understand the importance of emotional expression rather than suppression. However, the consequences of not having our emotional needs met would have imprinted on us and, in many cases, been carried into adulthood as trauma and Adverse Childhood Experiences (ACEs). (We will look at ACEs in chapter 6.)

As adults, there are many ways to overcome and heal our childhood experiences. Through neuroscience and our understanding of neuroplasticity, we now know that, as much as our early life experiences have shaped our brain (and subsequent behaviours, addictions and general wellbeing), we can create new neural connections and responses and therefore new outcomes. We *can* break the cycles and learn a different way of being.

Meditation

Scientists are now starting to research the effects of this ancient practice. First believed to be practiced in India in the Vedic and/or early Hindu schools, it is thought that Chinese Taoist and Indian Buddhist traditions developed their own versions of meditation practices. Recent research from Harvard University cited in the journal *Psychiatry Research* shows that meditation can change the structures of the brain by increasing the conical thickness in the hippocampus which, alongside other roles, regulates emotions. If meditation can regulate emotions, it can support us on our path to recovering from people pleasing. The same report also shows that regular meditation decreases the volume of the amygdala. So, the part of the brain that initiates our body's response to fear, stress and anxiety can shrink, therefore helping to minimise the impact that our early experiences have on us in adulthood. In addition, it's being revealed that meditation can help to reduce stress hormones and, in fact, increases DHEA which may help to curtail depression and adrenal fatigue.

(*Source:* https://www.health.harvard.edu/mind-and-mood/mindfulness-meditation-practice-changes-the-brain.)

Yoga Nidra, an ancient practice of deep conscious relaxation featuring guided meditation, allows the parasympathetic nervous system (the rest and digest system) to rest and recharge and elicit the relaxation response – crucial when we have experienced trauma, stress and other negative experiences that have caused fear-based responses.

***

My **Yoga Nidra MP3**, as well as the other resources mentioned throughout this book, can be accessed here:

www.soulconfidence.co.uk/ditch-the-people-pleaser-resources.

2
Raising People Pleasers

Let me tell you the story of a 'bossy' and precocious child. Spoiler alert: it's me. Now, this young girl was born, as you were, brimming with confidence – totally free, expressive, and in touch with every part of herself. She was the first child; a girl who said what she wanted, felt what she felt, and did what she felt like. A girl who felt deeply and who expressed herself freely. Except, of course, that she was labelled 'too bossy' and 'precocious' by the adults around her, all within earshot or directly to her face. It would seem the world didn't much like assertive young girls.

I saw the injustice in my world. I made signs and fundraised and joined charities. I was a vegetarian, joined WWF (the wildlife charity, not the wrestling federation!), and stood up for what I believed was right.

I campaigned in my home for my mum to stop smoking by plastering 'No Smoking Zone' posters over the car and house. (It paid off 20 years later when she did finally stop.)

Old before my time, I was wiser than what was expected for someone in their single digits, but young enough to be expected to blindly respect everything someone older than me said. (I learned this when my mum was called in to speak with my primary school teacher about my 'attitude' problem.) Thus, a constriction appeared for this highly sensitive child.

Being much older, I now know that sensitivity is a gift – a gift that contains so many superpowers. However, when you are eight and you don't know how to deal with your emotions (or everyone else's), when you don't know that you can pick up on everyone's energy or what having clairsentience means, sensitivity doesn't feel like a gift. When it is not nurtured like a gift it quickly becomes a burden.

Instead of embracing her sensitivity and seeing it for the gift that it was (had she realised that indeed it *was* a gift), 8-year-old Kara was thinking, 'All these older people are saying that being a bossy girl is bad and I have been told I am bossy. They hate me saying what I think or not following the line. I have been told repeatedly that adults are to be listened to and obeyed.' The voices and opinions of others are internalised as shame, so we very quickly learn to suppress our 'flaws'.

I made a conscious decision to fit in, to adapt, to become less of this and more of that. Though I must say that, despite learning how to fit in, I still popped out of that box frequently – you cannot keep a bossy and precocious kid down for that long, even when society dictates otherwise.

I hear adults say to their kids, 'Be quiet when adults are talking,' or they're not listening or being present to their children. No judgement here – it's not possible to be present 100% of the time. But we can create a relationship based on mutual respect, trust and compassion. The old adage 'children should be seen and not heard' doesn't fit with a more respectful approach to child-rearing, however, this attitude towards children still remains. We've seen this need to 'quash' the voice and spirit of children and young people happen on a larger scale, the outpouring of bile (notably by adults) towards the younger climate justice activists being the perfect example.

'How dare they challenge our generation?' 'What does a 16 year old know!' 'They should be in school learning not protesting.'

This is so dismissive and closed-minded. The misogyny, childism and ridiculousness of people thinking that, because they are older, they are automatically assumed wiser. And not only that but expecting young people to suppress who they are to make the adults around them feel more comfortable (and oftentimes, superior). You might have read a few more books, have more qualifications and life experience, and be the model tax-paying citizen, but this doesn't mean that you know better. Let young people be. In other words, let them express themselves. Yes, as a guardian, parent, or teacher you have a responsibility for younger people's welfare – health, safety, wellbeing, security - but it is not your place to censor or mould them into versions of what is sanitised and palatable by your standards. Young people do not have to learn how to people please. They do not exist to meet your needs or approval. And if we're talking about having a responsibility for their safety, let's ensure that we're including emotional safety too. Learning to ignore your own feelings and needs, and learning to stuff down emotions, does not allow one to feel emotionally safe. While this is a survival strategy to create the illusion of safety, many of us are now (as adults) having to undo much of that conditioning and heal from the traumas and mental health issues that arose as a result.

It is essential for all of our consciousness and the survival of this planet that our children do not repeat this cycle. Surely, one of the reasons the planet is in so much trouble is that children get 'trained' in how to fit in as young adults and no longer challenge the status quo?

I have zero desire for my child to people please. I love how kind and generous he is, and I love that he is also his own person. He has not been trained in 'how to be nice', but as parents we model respect and kindness and encourage him to think about his role in the world and society. We talk about racism, privilege, and society. We also encourage his innate kindness and consideration, and give him the space to be all of who he is. I talk about gratitude and appreciation with him. We ask him not to snatch or make demands, while understanding that he is young and learning all the time. We know as parents we are going to do it all imperfectly.

Being hyper aware of the stories around people pleasing, I see it in children a lot, especially girls. There is too much focus put on whether they are 'performing' how they should. Too many girls are told 'be nice' from an early age, then when they hit teens they are told it doesn't matter if people like them or not. By that point, any positive messages are drowned out by the indoctrination of our current society.

I would love to think Generation Z can grow up thinking people pleasing is not part of life, and being nice is not something to strive for. Instead, their inner qualities of kindness, love and generosity can lead the way.

If you do not want the children in your life to grow up people pleasing, then how are you modelling that? Are you being a people pleaser around them? If you are, it is time to do the work. For your growth, it is essential that you learn how to unpack your people pleasing stories, habits and behaviours so that you can tap back into your inner wisdom.

To start, you must re-discover what your story is – where, when and why you made a decision to people please in the first place. Identifying this means you can put the proverbial finger on it and understand yourself (and your behaviours) in a deeper way. That awareness and understanding gives you compassion; from compassion comes insight and from insight comes choice – the choice to continue people pleasing ... or not.

3
People Pleasing at Home

People pleasing in the home is rife, showing up as the (often unspoken) expectations of you (and your role) in the home, including the emotional well-being of everyone and the day-to-day running of the household. As people pleasers, we take on the tasks, not wishing to complain or ask for help, which often leads to resentment and strained relationships. Note that people-pleasing in the home is very much tied to binary gender stereotypes and expectations; resentment can brew on both sides.

Who bears the weight of the majority of the unseen or invisible labour in your home? Aside from the practical duties you do, it's important that you get clear on what invisible tasks you do also.

When I wrote my list, it looked like this:

- Help Arthur get ready before school

- Arrange appointments for Arthur – dentist, doctor, homeopath

- Keep on top of the laundry

- Make sure the cat is healthy

- Arrange our holiday plans

- Roughly, know everyone's timetable for each week

- Liaise with letting agent regarding the house we are in

Now, my partner and I have a 50/50 relationship with the practicalities – he does the cooking, is a father to his child (not a babysitter, he takes full responsibility of being a 50/50 caregiver), takes the bins out, and helps with the laundry.

I do not feel put upon or resentful in our home life. I do not do cooking or meal planning, so that is a huge chunk of labour taken away. We share cleaning and tidying. My partner takes the initiative and puts things away, and gets things done without me 'nagging'. At the same time, when I actually sat with how much time and energy of mine is used up in the minutia of those invisible tasks, I was surprised.

Recognising this and talking about it is key – having that recognition and a term to define it makes a world of difference. Acknowledging that you have a list of 'to-dos' and that a huge chunk of it is 'invisible' labour means you can start examining which of those tasks are pleasing you, and which are pleasing others.

If you are doing most of the invisible labour in your home and are feeling resentful about it, then you are people pleasing.

Be aware of invisible tasks like:

- Keeping the peace all the time in the house

- Organising everyone else's timetables

- Being the one who everyone off-loads onto, emotionally

- Being the one who buys all the gifts for all occasions

How are you feeling about them? Do you do them because you like to do them, or because you feel you 'have' to?

Reflection Point:

Write out your list – all the to-dos you do daily including the invisible labour and unseen actions. Go through that list and work out what is really weighing you down. Pick at least one and find a way to stop doing it, get support with it, or start working on a plan to let it go.

4
InnerFEARfreaks

When you examine people-pleasing in your day-to-day life, you need to understand the innerFEARfreaks and how they influence the ways you interact with the world. If nothing else, you will gain a sense of relief for knowing that it's not 'just you'. Having facilitated communities on and offline for over 10 years now, the biggest relief can be felt when someone hears you say, 'I feel like this ... One of my stories is ....' Every time, there is someone else in the room who thinks, 'Holy shit, I feel like that too. I have that story.'

As much as we think we're alone and our story is unique, we are far more connected than we realise. So insidious is people-pleasing that you probably have much more common ground with people than you think! It's a bit like social anxiety. We feel anxious in certain social situations, assuming that the people we're mingling with are super confident and in control. Yet they too are experiencing social anxiety, themselves wearing a mask of confidence and bravado to hide it. There is so much power when we share our feelings and experiences, giving others permission to drop the mask and create a deeper connection.

This book is focused on the people pleaser who, for me, has been my dominant innerFEARfreak in many situations. However, there are four others which interweave with the people pleaser. Knowing them, understanding them, and working to integrate them are paramount to feeling connection, abundance, joy and peace – when they are unacknowledged, they run amok and block the deeper experiences that come with presence.

The InnerFEARfreaks are worthy of their own book. What follows is a summary to help you begin this exploratory work. (If you'd like to take it further, I'll tell you how at the end of this chapter.)

Alongside the people pleaser, the innerFEARfreaks are:

1) The Control Freak

2) The Drama Queen

3) The Perfectionist

4) The Inner Rebel/Unheard Child

The Control Freak

The Control Freak is possibly one of the easiest to identify, as the need to control is something everyone experiences in some way or another. Needing to know how things will pan out, wanting someone to behave in a certain way, fear of things not going how you want, or worrying about things that have gone wrong before are very much tied in with our need for certainty (and therefore our need for safety, as discussed in the previous chapter).

If your Control Freak is dominant, you will notice you are clenched and holding a lot of tension in your body. You might be permanently poised to do something and find it hard to switch off. You will be stage-managing joy but actually leaving very little room for it via spontaneity.

Understanding where our control tendencies and stories came from and what they mean to you will release some of that need to control. The antidote is to trust and surrender – very hard when your Control Freak is dominant. The truth is, we cannot control anything or anyone outside of us, and trying to uses up a lot of energy. Getting comfortable with uncertainty – however much this goes against our conditioning – will help you to lean into trust and surrender.

People-pleasing is a form of control, and control is a form of people-pleasing. What the Control Freak can give you - through understanding, awareness and release of control - is profound trust and space to allow the unexpected to come through and the bigger plan to unfold.

The Drama Queen

The Drama Queen can be the loudest of all the innerFEARfreaks. Thriving on things going wrong, catastrophising, getting a kick out of being the victim – she never breaks the victim cycle.

When your Drama Queen is dominant you will be in your head a lot and stuck in an endless loop of conversation, typically about things that haven't happened yet but make you feel incredibly angry. Ever played an imaginary scenario over and over in your head until you're so worked up … yet nothing has actually happened? That's your Drama Queen! You may find your energy is ungrounded and that you react to everything.

There is very little peace when your Drama Queen is dominant. Being able to unpack the stories and experiences that have created the cycle of hurt and disappointment will lead to space to be present and to choose to respond rather than react. You move from a place of reactivity to boundless love and compassion for you and everyone around you.

The Perfectionist

The Perfectionist is all about the need for things to be just so (and is very closely connected to the Control Freak). Even more than that is the need to meet some impossibly perfect standard. This could be to do with your appearance, body, work, how you are as a parent, partner or friend – there are a myriad of places the Perfectionist shows up. There is a lot of resentment locked into the Perfectionist. Understanding where the specific breed of perfect comes from for you means that you can rein in your Perfectionist and, instead, enjoy imperfection.

When your Perfectionist is dominant, you might have an inner dialogue saying things like:

'I need to wait till I get x before I can do this or before I am ready.'
'I want to look like this before I do that.'
'I need to know I've got this 100 per cent right before I start.'

These thoughts keep you stuck in compete and compare,

and/or procrastination.

If you hear your Perfectionist as dialogue in your head, it is important to get clear on whose voice it is. Is it yours or someone else's? Where do you feel tension in your body when you feel the need for things to be 'perfect'?

Your Perfectionist often goes hand in hand with the people pleaser, meaning that you set (and strive for) idealistic goals and expectations, while simultaneously disconnecting from what you need and want. Even when you reach your goals, you never feel how you want to.

By accepting your Perfectionist, you are gifted the ability to fall deeply in love with yourself and feel acceptance on every level. The antidote is imperfect action: just do something imperfectly, whatever it is.

The Inner Rebel/Unheard Child

One of the most complex of the innerFEARfreaks is often identified as your inner child.

She might come out when you feel

- unsafe

- unheard

- unseen

Any unhealed mother/father wounds (covered in more detail in Section 2) are connected to our inner child. When you feel in pain, it's a sign that your inner child needs something. When you act up, this is often a sign that your inner rebel needs something she is not getting. Your inner child is fuelled each and every time you supress an emotion or let one of your needs go unmet. (Unmet needs = classic sign of people pleasing.)

When you sit with the Inner Rebel/Unheard Child, she reminds you that YOU need your love, attention and respect. Sit with yourself and be with whatever emotions you have. At times when you do make mistakes, remember that you are human; cut out the self-shaming and treat yourself with real compassion.

While the 7-Step Exploration throughout this book is intended for your people pleaser, you can also use it for each of the other innerFEARfreaks when they are running the show. If there is only one thing you do when reading this book, make it the 7-Step Exploration (though, of course, you'll gain value from all of the resources within these pages).

Using this process doesn't mean you'll become your

innerFEARfreak. But you will be fully present to all parts of you, and access your connection to your Higher Self/Intuition/God in the most powerful way. If you do not acknowledge your innerFEARfreaks and work with them, then you are allowing them to run the show from a place of pain, fear and past experiences. Your ability to go deeper and deeper with them each time will bring you back to the present.

***

The innerFEARfreaks are far more complex, deep and nuanced than what has been summarised in this chapter. If you want to explore this further and do the deepest of inner work, have a look here to see what programmes I am currently running: www.soulconfidence.co.uk

Section 2

People Pleasing ... In Relationships

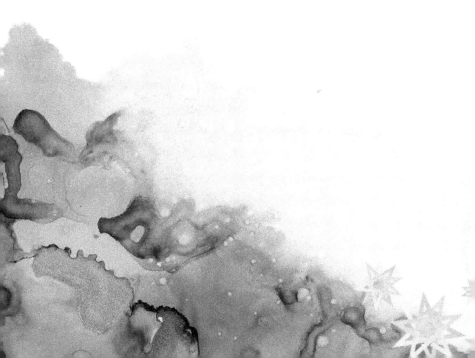

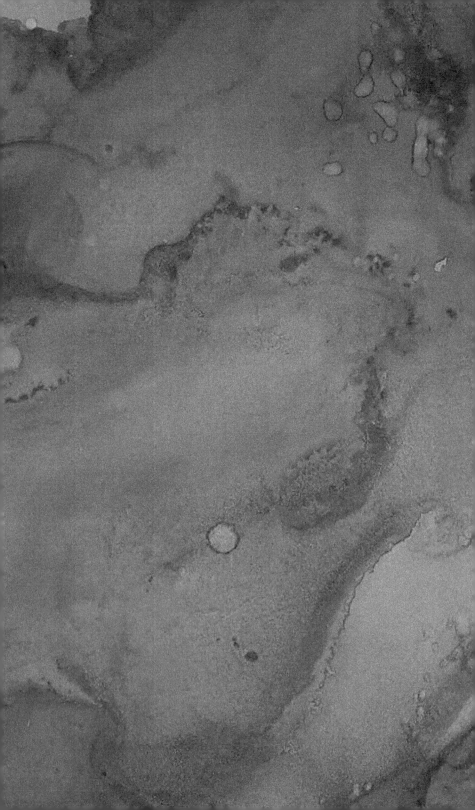

In this section we will cover one of the aspects of life that brings us both joy and pain, often in equal measure: relationships. From family to friendships and our most intimate of relationships, we crave belonging. As discussed in the previous section, our need for belonging can often come at the cost of our own happiness and wellbeing, particularly when we trade our needs for those of others.

We all want to be accepted, seen, heard, loved and understood, however, much of the conditioning and pain we take into adulthood comes as a result of not feeling those things throughout our childhood and adolescence. Typically, to ensure our sense of belonging (and survival), we over compensate for our unmet needs by overindulging the needs of those in our relationships – classic people pleasing territory!

People-pleasing makes our acceptance and sense of belonging conditional. It means we are only accepted and belong 'when' we behave and relate to others in a specific way. So, where do we stand if our relationships are built around pleasing others (or, indeed, expecting others to please us)? And what part do we play in shaping our relationships?

Read the chapters in this section with an open heart and mind. Reflect and use the tools and practices to get a deeper understanding of how and why you people please. Ultimately, true belonging and connection starts from within.

5
Family

Perhaps one of the juiciest topics to dissect with people-pleasing is family. From being a mum who puts her kids first to being 'nice' to keep the peace – there is a lot of people-pleasing that goes on within families. As children, we are rewarded for our 'good' behaviour, and punished for being 'bad'. Perhaps you've been emotionally blackmailed or threatened by a family member to meet their demands and expectations, or invited people you've never met to your wedding at the request of your relatives. Isn't it fascinating that, in a space where we 'should' automatically belong, much of our belonging and acceptance is conditional? No wonder people-pleasing has become synonymous with family life!

Reflection Point:
Take a moment to consider your family. Where do you people please, and who do you people please with? Do you know why?

Family dynamics can be the most complex (and toxic) of all relationships. Intergenerational trauma continues down the lineage, often rooted in mother (and father) wounds that are repeated until the cycle is broken.

The Mother Wound

'The Mother Wound is the pain of being a woman passed down through generations of women in patriarchal cultures. And it includes the dysfunctional coping mechanisms that are used to process that pain.'~ Bethany Webster

Many women I know (clients and friends) who class themselves as people-pleasers have (or have had) a complicated relationship with their mother. I'm no exception. My relationship with my mum has comprised a myriad of fractured emotions. As well as experiencing my own pain from childhood, I can now look back at my mother's experience and see the ways that she struggled too. For example, I can now see that she put her own needs last a lot of the time. I can still hear - and more importantly, feel - the impact of her words: 'I never do what I want, I always put you kids first.' Seeing her bringing up three children with this ringing in my ears led to a lot of guilt. Without a doubt, the feeling of preventing your mother from having the life she really wanted is heavy. When we have a people-pleasing woman who we model our world on in our formative years, becoming a people-pleaser ourselves can be inevitable. Additionally, when you have a parent who projects their dissatisfaction and unhappiness, you learn to feel responsible for their feelings. You devise ways to make their life easier and happier, thus entering a co-dependent people-pleasing relationship dynamic. Once I realised the potentially toxic impact this dynamic could have on my own child, I was determined to break the cycle. The Mother Wound *has* to be healed. If I can avoid passing that burden on to my children, I will. I know you do not want anyone in your life to feel that burden either.

Patty says: 'I have no doubt that the idea of people-pleasing began as a very young child. I was the fourth of five siblings and my parents were very strict. I grew up in New York in a very Irish, Catholic neighbourhood and attended Catholic school. I learned to live by rules and, so long as you followed the rules, you would be rewarded. My parents were not very loving parents. They were always fighting.

We did not have a very warm, loving environment to grow up in. It was a kind of every-man-for-himself atmosphere. So, as a survival mechanism, I learned how to receive love by doing things that made people happy, and in return found some self-worth, love and attention. The beginning of people pleasing. This idea of people-pleasing was beyond family; it also included teachers, friends, neighbours etc.'

This is a good place to look at the importance of the primary caregiver's role on a child and whether that influences the need to please as you grow older. Bowlby's Theory of Attachment (developed and refined through the 20th century) cites three attachment behaviours: secure, anxious-resistant and avoidant. Mary Ainsworth developed these theories following studies with young infants and their primary caregivers to record the reaction of the children when their primary caregiver a) left the research space and b) returned. If the infant got visibly upset upon their caregiver leaving but was easily comforted on their return, this was classed as secure attachment. If the infant was distressed when their caregiver left and was hard to soothe on their return, and exhibiting conflicting behaviours, this was classed as anxious-resistant. If the infant was not overly distressed on their primary care giver leaving and actively avoided contact with them on their return, this was classed as avoidant. (To explore this further, I recommend the book *Patterns of Attachment* (Psychology Press & Routledge Classic Editions), by Mary Ainsworth.)

From the 1980s onwards, there has been significant research into whether these attachment behaviours as children affect our adult relationships. If we consider how the brain works (as discussed in chapter 1), a piece of research in 2018 on adult attachment theory suggests they do: 'If we assume that adult relationships are attachment relationships, it is possible that children who are secure as children will grow up to be secure in their romantic relationships. Or, relatedly, that people who are secure as adults in their relationships with their parents will be more likely to forge secure relationships with new partners.'

(www.labs.psychology.illinois.edu/~rcfraley/attachment.htm - R. Chris Fraley Adult Attachment Theory and Research A Brief Overview.)

The primary caregiver does not have to be the mother but predominately it is. Attachment theory was based on the principal that young mammals are not able to feed or protect themselves; they are dependent on their primary caregiver to meet these needs. If the primary caregiver is nearby and accessible (which, in humans, also means emotionally available and self-regulated), the child feels safe to play and explore feeling secure. When the primary caregiver isn't available to meet their needs, the child enters a physiological state of survival; it doesn't feel safe.

People-pleasing is something we learn in order to 'survive'. As Patty mentioned earlier, learning to receive love by doing things that made people happy was a survival mechanism. With a lack of secure attachment, she devised a way to receive the self-worth, love and attention that she needed to gain an illusional sense of safety.

Children who feel secure are able to show all their emotions without having to hide them; it's safe for them to do so. Anxious-resistant or avoidant children tend to repress their emotions or be overwhelmed and all-consumed by them. As a people-pleaser, you may recognise these in yourself.

Rhona shared some of her story with me, and it's one that may resonate with you. From early childhood, Rhona was constantly compared to her cousin by her mum. Her cousin was, in Rhona's words, 'Perfect in every way, behaviour, school, grades, looks –

everything! I spent years wishing I was her and could be as good as her in my mum's eyes.'

How sad that a young girl spent years of her life wishing she was someone else. How many young people do this? How many young people grow up wishing they were someone else - someone more intelligent, prettier, chattier, funnier, better behaved - in order to make their parents happy? By being compared to her cousin, Rhona lost who she was (albeit temporarily) in order to please her mum. Woah - what a tough family dynamic! What was Rhona's mum's motivation in this? Was she actually happier once Rhona moulded herself into a more acceptable version?

Rhona's mum would have had to do some major digging into how she felt about herself before she could become satisfied with anything. To be unable to accept your daughter for who she is or, at the very least, to understand how damaging comparison is for your child requires a huge level of awareness. When parents are unaware and unconscious, this is the result. Your child has to do the work for themselves, for you, and after following generations before.

If Rhona had not done the healing work, her life would be very different now. Instead of being aware of her people pleaser, she would be unconscious of her actions and to how she feels physically, emotionally and spiritually. Without doing the work to let go of the people pleaser, she would be holding onto a lot of tension in her body. For example, when you hold on to people-pleasing, your shoulders, back and hips can feel tight with tension. Emotionally, she would be like a jack-in-the-box, holding onto resentment, overwhelm, and never able to express herself fully – until something would set her off and she could jump out, full of unprocessed anger. Spiritually, she would disconnect and not meet self-fulfilment (or self-actualisation as per Maslow's Hierarchy of Needs in chapter 1) which is part of our purpose in this human experience.

Of course, the impact of people pleasing doesn't stop with us. It ripples to the people around us, especially our children. Without doing the healing work, the impact on Rhona's children would have been huge. They would have grown up picking up her people pleasing habits, or casually accepted (typically through unconscious cues) that females have a duty to put their needs last.

This, again, reinforces two points:

1) How important it is for your physical, emotional and spiritual growth to let go of people pleasing. If you don't,

dis-ease may manifest in your body. Your emotional health will suffer, you'll struggle to connect to your intuition, and you'll miss out on opportunities to express your purpose.

2) How important it is to let go of people pleasing for the young people in your life (now and in the future) – people pleasing is one legacy we don't want to leave behind! If you do not do the inner work, the younger people around you will continue the cycle.

Luckily for Rhona, she was aware of her behaviours and, when she became a mum, was committed to doing the work so as not to pass this destructive pattern onto her children. Are you willing to do the same?

Reflection Point:
Can you reflect on the relationship with your mother – was there any similar patterns between you? Can you identify the people pleasing cycle within your family?

6
Father Relationship

When I did some social research and asked, 'When was the idea of people pleasing reinforced consciously or unconsciously within you?' 90% of women traced their people pleasing back to wanting the love, approval, and validation that they did not get from their father – that steady, kind, unconditional masculine presence was missing or skewed for many people-pleasers.

As Shelley shares: 'From a very young age, my emotional needs were not met. My father continued to put me down and tell me l was thick and stupid. I was desperately trying to get my father to love me. My self-esteem was very low, and l assumed, at a young age, that l was unlovable. I spent years trying to please others and get them to like me.'

If your need to be liked and approved of by a strong masculine was missing, you might find yourself (as an adult) putting everyone else's needs before your own. You may seek a 'father-figure' in a relationship and do everything you can to please and keep him. You may enter a relationship with someone who has similar traits to your father, even if they are abusive. You may run yourself ragged in the constant hope that you will get the love, approval and validation that was missing. The direction and depth that takes will depend on whether that masculine presence was missing, distant, disapproving or abusive.

Without doing the work to unpack your people-pleasing story and to understand your triggers, the cycle is set to repeat again. And again. And again.

I was in that cycle of seeking someone to give me the love, approval and validation that I missed from my father. My father was a mixture of abusive, at times distant, and at other times obsessively interested in me. The sexual abuse was covert. The emotional abuse was intense. For a long time, I bounced from semi-relationship to semi-relationship with men who were a mixture of distant and obsessively interested in me. I would attract men who were all over me one minute and cold and distant the next. I also had a habit of choosing men who were emotionally unavailable and then spend time and energy thinking of how to get their attention. My lowest point was when I went back to someone who had date raped me. I did not consider myself to be a victim; I thought those relationships were what I was worthy of. I was also adept at hiding warning signs from others – well trained from childhood and only painting the picture to friends that I wanted them to see.

That cycle was set to repeat until I was willing to break it. I had to experience a lot of discomfort to do that. However, that discomfort was better than the alternative.

More research is emerging now about the impact of father-child relationships. Learning about Adverse Childhood Experiences (ACEs) put a lot in perspective about the impact my father had had on me (though ACEs relate to all parental figures).

The understanding of ACEs began with ten questions based around experiences like abuse, domestic violence, lack of safety, and substance misuse in childhood. More questions have subsequently extended the profile. When I did the initial ten questions, my score was eight. My score was quite revelatory, although I was well aware of the unhealthy, dysfunctional environment I was raised in.

A third of all mental health conditions in adults are directly related to adverse childhood experiences. Having four or more ACEs can have a significant psychological impact on you as a child and, when carried into adulthood, can lead to serious health issues, substance misuses, and more. Without awareness and the appropriate therapy needed to heal, the cycle may continue.

As formative as our relationships with our parents or primary care givers are, it is possible to create the resilience, secure attachment and self-love that was eroded through an unhealthy childhood. As mentioned in chapter 1, neuroplasticity means that we can create new neural connections in our brain and, subsequently, more positive outcomes. We have already looked at the incredible healing power of meditation and mindfulness. Having experienced ACEs with no idea of these concepts at the time, my ways to create resilience, secure attachment and self-love as an adult have included:

- **Therapy.** This was crucial for my emotional recovery. It remains crucial for my wellbeing. It provides me with a safe space to talk, cry, and heal.

- **Yoga.** My lifeline for my reconnection to my body through re-learning how to breathe and how to open my body back up. Still my favourite way to come back to myself.

- **Various energy-healing modalities**. These supported my vital reconnection to Source.

I talk in my work about your internal and external support systems. Both are equally important and support your healing and growth. Externals include therapy, counselling, and energy healers. It's so important that you find the right person to work with. Take your time and listen to your intuition about who is going to support you. Get a few consultations before you decide on a therapist, go to a drop-in class before you pre-book a block of yoga classes, and check in with the reviews and credentials of the energy healers you are looking to work with. And, perhaps more importantly, do ensure that your therapist is trauma-informed, or at least has a very good working knowledge of trauma. This may sound obvious, however, you'd be surprised how many people do not have this knowledge and awareness, and who consequently risk re-traumatising their clients.

7
Parenting

We've already touched upon parenting and how our people pleasing can impact our children, and the subsequent patterns of behaviour that are repeated if we do not do the inner work. We've looked at evolutionary science and people pleasing as a survival strategy, and we've considered the difference between people pleasing and co-operation, as well as raising children who are kind versus 'nice'. In this chapter, we are going to take the focus away from your children and look at parenting from a different perspective: you and your *role* as a parent.

Let's be honest – parenting isn't always easy. Some of us find a new found confidence and sense of purpose when we have children while others lose our confidence (and ourselves). Many of us enter into parenthood completely unprepared for the reality which rarely matches our pre-baby romanticised notions of how it will be. There's nothing quite like birthing new life into the world to force you to face your demons!

Nowadays, unless we choose an alternative approach, healthcare professionals have a lot more input and control over our children (and our body) from the moment we discover we're pregnant. This isn't a criticism, more a reflection of how times (and medicine) have changed. Where once we would have primarily been guided by our natural instincts and intuition, now we look to the outside and the plethora of often conflicting advice and information. We stop trusting ourselves and instead put our trust in the hands of professionals and relative strangers. From a people pleasing perspective, this can look like making decisions based on others' opinions rather than listening to our innate wisdom, needs and desires. It can look like doubting your intuition while never questioning others' advice.

Later on, people pleasing can look like getting your child Christened because a relative expects you to (even though you aren't part of the Christian faith); or not setting boundaries when your baby is born, instead resentfully allowing everyone to visit when what you really want is bonding time with your baby.

It's easy to get the message that everything we're doing as a parent is wrong. This is tough for the people pleaser who needs constant validation that we're doing things right. Instead, we often find ourselves crippled with self-doubt while trying to create the façade that we have everything together!

People pleasing as a parent takes many forms:

- Not advocating for your child when confronted by family members, friends, other parents and teachers about their behaviour

- Trying to micro-manage and control your child's behaviour so that you can control other people's perception of them and, perhaps more pertinent, other people's perception of you and your parenting ability (hello, innerCONTROLfreak!)

- Saying yes to playdates when you want to say no, or not wanting to leave a party early because you don't want to appear rude (even though your highly-sensitive introverted child is desperate for some quiet time!)

- Hiding who you really are with other parents (and likely drinking to excess to numb social anxiety at social events!)

- Sacrificing your integrity and values just so you can 'fit in' with other parents

- Spending Christmas and other 'special' occasions with extended family when you really want to spend it alone with your partner and children

- Performative parenting, i.e. changing your parenting style because people are watching

- Not speaking up against friends/family who are making problematic comments in front of your children, e.g. about their appearance/weight, racist or homophobic comments etc

Advocating and being the voice for your child is perhaps one of the most difficult things to do as a people pleaser. On the one hand, as deeply sensitive, compassionate beings, you know that your child is worthy and deserving of respect, and to be accepted and nurtured for who they are, warts and all. On the other hand, your need to be liked and accepted means that sometimes it's easier to follow the status quo without challenge. However, children need to know that at least one adult in their life has their back, no matter what. This doesn't mean that they aren't held accountable for their actions. But it does mean that they are approached with empathy and compassion, and are given permission to make mistakes. Children are, after all, human – just like us! Also, by advocating for our children (and by our children bearing witness to this), they learn to advocate for themselves. The more they can advocate for themselves, the less they'll look to others for approval.

Reflection Point:

Looking at the list above, can you identify where you have people pleased as a parent? Why do you want to move away from this now?

8
Friendships

As we mature, through adolescence and into our early twenties, our friendships become as important as our family relationships as we are able to discern and choose who we spend time with. Friendships - at their best - can nurture and uplift you, giving you emotional support as well as allowing you to reciprocate that emotional support. However, friendships can sometimes feel one-sided or based on unfair expectations, especially if your people pleaser is very active in your relationship!

Rachel shared: 'I would always go out of my way to do things for people but always felt like I never got the same back from friends. I had a deep feeling of anger in me but I never knew why or where it came from. I would always snap or make passive aggressive comments, and then feel really stupid and stew on them for ages after.'

Relatable, right? How many times do you go out of your way because you are trying to please someone? It might seem like you are being 'nice' but actually it's not coming from a truthful place. This is when we need to be radically honest with ourselves about our motive and intention. For example; you offer to let your friend stay for a few days while her house is being repainted. If your motive is, 'My mate is going to be so grateful and like me so much more for this,' rather than, 'I want to help, and it would be great to spend a bit of extra time together,' then you are attaching to an outcome dependent on something you can't control. It is *you* trying to control that person. The second motive is coming from your desire to help. So, better to not be 'nice' and instead be truthful. If you offer something, let it come from your truth.

Of course, if you feel you have offered something with a truthful, authentic motivation and you do not feel appreciated, there could be a boundary to be looked at. An honest conversation explaining how you feel, or making a decision to do something different in the future, will strengthen your choice not to people please. This is not about being a doormat or about feeling unappreciated. It is a choice you make to show up the way that feels good to you in each friendship.

Going above and beyond, at times, can be a beautiful thing, but check in if you feel a sense of obligation, or that it's being demanded of you. If you are feeling obligated or in demand, it is coming from a place of expectation.

There are friendships where you may have played that role for so long that an expectation has been made on you to be a certain way. Changing this dynamic might be disruptive – some people won't appreciate the 'new' you. Keeping it, though, is destructive. I can promise you that, as you keep working through the 7-Step Exploration, you won't want to stay in your people pleasing role to maintain the status quo.

In chapter 1 we briefly touched on the people-pleasing dynamics – victim, martyr (rescuer) and, for the dynamic to work, the perpetrator (oppressor). This is known as the drama triangle. The drama triangle is a model of social interaction that maps destructive interactions occurring between people, particularly in conflict. We all assume each 'role' at various stages in our lives.

In some friendships, especially those where we have set ourselves up as the victim or martyr from the beginning, our 'friend' assumes the role of the perpetrator. This doesn't mean that we experience abuse from them, however, they hold the power and control within the friendship. Their desires and needs dominate your own which, quite frankly, plays straight into the hands of your people pleaser! It becomes quite the reciprocal relationship – your friend enables your need to please while you validate their oppressive power. In these friendships, you may 'shrink' or blur into the background while your friend takes centre stage. When you're both single and dating, you take a backseat, assuming that everyone will like your friend anyway. You're reluctant to voice your opinion, instead agreeing with theirs, or find that you don't even have a voice.

As you grow in confidence, find your voice, and start to value yourself more, these are the very relationships that begin to fall away. The dynamic changes; you are no longer the martyr *or* the victim (and the 'perpetrator' needs either to survive). So, you become surplus to requirements. The end of a friendship is tough, even if the relationship was unhealthy. With a shared history, and a whole identity built around it, the loss of a friend can bring up feelings of grief, anger, rejection and betrayal. No matter the relationship or circumstances, allow yourself to feel *all* the feelings.

It is now *your* decision to choose not to people please. As you will see in the intimate relationships chapter, if someone wants you to be happy, they will respect the changes you make. If not, it wasn't a supportive, reciprocal relationship.

Learning to release the expectations that you have put on yourself to be that 'likeable' or 'acceptable' someone means forgiving other people who you have people pleased for. Some people will have gained a lot from you with little or nothing in return. I want to be clear: this is not a get-enlightened-quick scheme – this work takes effort and time. So, please be gentle on yourself. The first step for any kind of recovering people pleaser is awareness. Once you're clear on your origin stories and become present to the impact people pleasing is having on your life, the next step is to understand, on every level, that the validation you are desperately seeking through people pleasing is fleeting and empty. It's not worth the sacrifice. For me, I needed that validation because I did not like myself. I needed that validation because I didn't believe I was enough without it. Now we get to flip those beliefs and reconnect to the truth at the core of our very being: we *are* enough. And that includes you!

Reflection Point:

On a piece of paper, make three columns. In column one, write out a list of all the important relationships in your life. In column two, write whether you people please or not within that relationship. In column three, write down what you need to do to change that dynamic.

9
Intimate Relationships

While we often think of sex when we think of intimacy, what we really mean is closeness (we'll discuss sex in the next chapter!). Being intimate with someone means being vulnerable, allowing them into your heart and sharing *all* of you, even the dark and messy parts. Of course, this is like kryptonite for your people pleaser (and ego), as it means stepping out from behind the mask.

In my intimate relationship, this is where my people pleaser likes to hang out the most. Through extensive (and somewhat painful) research, I discovered that there are three layers to the people pleaser. For me, the understanding sunk in when I did the 7-Step Exploration – I realised that I had picked up people pleasing as a defence mechanism/coping strategy for being in a healthy and supportive relationship. Rather than allowing my truth to come out, people pleasing enabled me to stay 'safe' in the relationship by hiding the parts of me that I thought would be rejected.

The three layers are specific to intimate relationships, though you may recognise them in other relationships as well. You will see how people pleasing shows up through those layers, affecting communication, your levels of happiness, your ability to experience pleasure, and your overall wellbeing. I am focusing this section on how *you* feel. I will add, however, that a positive side effect is a better experience in the relationship for your partner. However, if the relationship isn't right or safe for you, then please don't stay and think you just need to do more work. I truly hope that if you aren't in the right relationship this chapter will help you realise that it is time to leave.

As you read about each layer, get clear on where you sit within each, and get ready to use the antidote – **Put Yourself First**.

The First Layer:

YOU ARE MORE IMPORTANT THAN I AM

This layer is putting the other person's needs above your own. This is the tricky starting point. When you become aware of your people pleaser, you will notice the places where your people pleaser shows up. When you become aware of your thoughts, actions and beliefs in your intimate relationship (or a potential one), you will see how you always put that person's needs before your own.

In this layer, you do not know how to articulate what you need. You will most likely be having communication issues in your intimate relationship and you will be pushing all those emotions down.

This is your reminder: Your self-worth can never be validated through anyone else. Take back your power, and stop waiting for someone else to make you feel better about anything. The first step to taking back your power in your intimate relationship is to peel back this first layer and apply the antidote – Put Yourself First.

Your partner (most likely) does *not* want you to second-guess what they want, and actually wants you simply to be you. If they do not want that, they are not the right person for you. This goes for EVERY relationship. If the person you are people pleasing sulks, stops talking to you, and demands that you go back to the 'old' you when you start using the people pleasing antidote, then they do not have your best interests. It is up to you to decide if your energy is best used on that relationship (or not).

The Second Layer:

I CAN ONLY BE HAPPY WITH YOU

Good old co-dependency. This is where you realise you are expecting all your fulfilment to come from your partner. You have lost sight of what it's like to have fun outside of your relationship, and there may be intense jealousy at the idea of your partner doing anything without you.

You will find yourself saying 'I'm fine' on a regular basis, which, as you know, is seldom the case. You know if you utter the words 'I'm fine' then it immediately means that you're not. At all. Using this phrase only serves to make you feel worse – you become a seething pool of unexpressed emotion, pushed way down and plastered over with stories of how you need to make the other person happy to be accepted. In this layer, although the emotions will spring up, you are not able to process them.

Again, you need to apply the antidote here – Put Yourself First. You need to be willing to discover how you can be happy *on your own*. Yes, it's possible, I PROMISE you! This could look like a period of time on your own, using your internal support systems to do what you need to. You most definitely need to process your emotions and your needs.

The Third Layer:

WHAT DO I ACTUALLY WANT FROM YOU + ME?

The third layer is all about sex and intimacy.

Opening myself up to intimacy was one of the most vulnerable things I have ever done. I avoided intimacy and instead used tactics to numb myself from being present with myself. These tactics meant I could never REALLY listen to what I needed and wanted in the moment. In this layer, the intimacy starts with you. How are you willing to get to know *you*?

I didn't even know how much of my energy was consumed with micro-managing everyone else's happiness until I started to unpick it, not as a martyr or victim, but as a person who deserves the utmost in love and compassion. And yes, without a doubt, love and compassion starts with how you listen and talk to YOU. Once you are in an amazing relationship with yourself, the people pleasing *has* to stop – you won't tolerate it for yourself anymore.

I think some of the biggest lessons I have learned and achievements I have made have been in my intimate relationship. Truthfully, it is messy and painful going through the layers … and then to be willing to go even deeper. The work never stops.

Being your wellbeing warrior is crucial to supporting yourself on your journey to ditching your people pleaser. You have to know what you need and when you need it to keep your 'bucket' full. Depletion and overwhelm will see you slipping back into the old patterns of people pleasing. Being your wellbeing warrior is bespoke to your body, breath and Soul. This means you need to get clear on what your Essential Me Time Maintenance (EMTM) looks like *every* day. EMTM incorporates your self-care, on and off the mat practice, plus your internal and external support systems. It also means self-talk and boundaries. You want your Essential Me Time Maintenance to support you throughout the month, and to work with your personal cycle and/or the moon cycle – as your energy changes and shifts, you need to work with that energy, not against it. Most importantly, while it is lovely to know yourself and what you need, none of that matters if you aren't actually doing it! Tap into your antidote - Put Yourself First - and set up your EMTM to do the things that make you feel good.

To support you, please download my **Daily Presence Practice**

MP3, which can be accessed here:

www.soulconfidence.co.uk/ditch-the-people-pleaser-resources

10
Love, Sex and Sexuality

I f we didn't receive the love and connection that we needed growing up, or were raised with an anxious or avoidant attachment, it's not uncommon to seek them through unhealthy means. Sex is something that can easily be 'traded' for love, however fleeting the moment.

While sex in itself isn't unhealthy – hey, it can be the most magical and pleasurable experience – when the intention behind it comes from a place of insecurity and need for validation, we can be left feeling empty and less lovable, often needing *more* sex to feel *more* lovable, thus entering a destructive cycle. We may find ourselves agreeing to sex acts that make us feel uncomfortable, or relationships that feel unsafe, simply to be liked (or loved) more. Overtime, we can develop a warped sense of sex which can impact our intimate relationships later on.

Love + Sex

Wrapped up in expectation and validation are love and sex. 10 years ago, I would have run away at the idea of sharing my feelings towards sex with you. I did not know how to do sex. Physical and emotional pain left me feeling trapped. I needed to numb myself to have sex, and I never had an orgasm. I was in total fear and believed that I was intrinsically broken. Love and sex to people pleasers is something we crave but equally fear. I think it's fair to assume that we all have a story around love and sex.

I was 16. I had just spent the night with my then boyfriend in a consensual sexual situation (I will spare you the teenage details). I felt utter shame. Disgust. Hatred. I shut down even further. The story started to go deeper. 'I am broken. I am wrong.' The first time I had sex I cried and cried. The physical pain was excruciating, and the wave of emotional pain was uncontrollable. I didn't know how to articulate what was happening. It wasn't a one-off. So, alcohol became an essential crutch to be 'normal' during sex aka to Not Be Sensitive. I wasn't able to articulate to others or myself the abuse I had experienced as a child. What followed in the coming years was date rape and a series of toxic relationships. I even went back to the partner who had date raped me. That was how institutionalised my people pleasing was.

The change happened when I started to train as a yoga teacher. I resisted meditation for as long as I could, as I knew I did not want to get quiet with myself. Then, one night, I realised I couldn't resist it any more. I was tired of constantly ignoring myself and drowning out everything. I meditated. And the words came: 'You were abused by your father when you were seven.' I broke down. For a couple of days, I was in a weird limbo of relief and despair. To know what I always knew and to be able to face it was both a confrontation and surrender. Counselling and therapy have supported me to release the trauma around the abuse, and to get to a point where I can rebuild my relationship around love and sex.

My relationship with my father could never be rebuilt. He rejected me time and time again, and the fear around that stayed when he left. For people pleasers to release the old stories around love and sex takes effort. To release the pain takes energy. Many of us have experienced trauma. It may not have been sexual trauma but, as a sensitive person, you will have absorbed trauma. By shutting down your sensitivity, that trauma would have been held in your body.

I am not a trauma therapist. I am not a therapist or counsellor. If any clients disclose to me that they have experienced abuse or trauma, I advise them to work with a trained professional. They have the essential techniques and training. How I support people, however, is by harnessing the power of their sensitivity - compassion, courage and connection - in work, purpose, relationships, and using their voice, and through connecting with their body, mind and soul. Many healing modalities focus on the mind, which has its place, of course. However, healing from trauma requires a somatic approach. If you don't work with a counsellor or trauma specialist, then I would advise using your breath - something we all have access to - as well as body work as part of your practice. This is what I do, even today. My practice is my helpline, my anchor – it got me through and gets me through so much.

When you connect with your breath - your breath that has been held for a very long time; the breath you suppress so that you can do all the things for everyone else - you release tension, stress, anxiety and fear. You re-learn to be present. As a people pleaser, it's imperative that you bring yourself back into the here and now. Using your breath, you can let go of the hold the past has on you, even just for a moment, and release the fear of the future. Your breath creates space in your body and mind, allowing you to access that deep unwavering love for yourself.

You can access my **Daily Breath MP3** at the following link: www.soulconfidence.co.uk/ditch-the-people-pleaser-resources

Reflection Point:
Observe your breath. How do you habitually breathe? Does anything change in your breath or body when you think of intimacy? Be curious and notice.

Love Languages

If you're familiar with the work of Gary Chapman, you will know that he has identified five languages that we speak (mostly non-verbally) that allow us to feel loved. Understanding our dominant love language and that of our partner can improve our communication and relationship. The five love languages are summarised below. If you would like to explore these in more depth, you can find out more in, *The 5 Love Languages*.

Words of Affirmation

This love language expresses love through positive words and includes verbal compliments and the simplest of praise. Negative words and criticism will harm a person with this dominant love language.

Quality Time

This love language is about undivided attention and being present to someone without distractions. Postponing time with or not being present to someone whose love language is quality time can be harmful.

Receiving Gifts

A meaningful or thoughtful gift makes someone with this dominant love language feel appreciated. They also tend to gift others as an expression of their love. Forgetting birthdays or not putting thought into a gift, which could be as simple as surprising them with their favourite bar of chocolate, can leave a person with this dominant love language feeling unappreciated.

Acts of Service

This love language expresses itself by doing things with positive intention and with your partner's happiness in mind. This doesn't include actions out of obligation or with a negative tone. Someone with this dominant love language will require their partner to be receptive of their service, and not too stubborn or independent to receive it.

Physical Touch

People with this love language feel connected and safe in a relationship through holding hands, hugging and kissing etc. A lack of physical touch can leave them touch-starved and feeling rejected.

As people pleasers, we are more likely to carry patterns of co-dependency within our relationships, making ourselves responsible for the needs and feelings of others. In terms of the love languages, relationships are strengthened when both partners reciprocate the love language of the other. If we make an effort to spend quality time with our partner, for example, but they don't honour our language of receiving gifts, communication breaks down, our needs are ignored, and we can become resentful.

Of course, we *all* need to take responsibility for our own needs, and for voicing when our needs are being neglected by our partner – we cannot expect anyone to read our mind! There is, however, a very fine line between co-dependency and interdependence, the latter meaning that we own our emotions, take responsibility for meeting our own needs (without putting the onus on everyone else to meet them) AND lean on our partner for emotional support. Relationships are (supposed to be) an equal partnership that requires give, take, and consideration on both sides. Knowing the language in which you most feel loved, and wanting your partner to understand and honour it, doesn't make you insecure or needy. It simply means that it's the expression that most resonates and enables you to communicate (and receive) love more effectively and authentically.

Michelle says: 'As a reformed people pleaser, my love language is affirmations. Growing up I was praised for my academic achievement and artistic skills. In truth, it was the only time that I heard anything positive said about me without some negative back-handed undertone (which, I'm sure, we can all resonate with as sensitives). So, I internalised this praise as love. My partner, meanwhile, needs physical touch to feel loved – not easy when I find touch sensory-overload a lot of the time. At one point, he and I had a breakdown in communication. I realised that neither of us was speaking the other's love language. While we're very interdependent and understand that we're not responsible for each other, we now consciously spend a little time each day to speak the other's love language. He gives me words of encouragement, especially when I'm feeling tired or down, and I show physical affection (albeit as much as I can physically tolerate).'

My love language is also words of affirmation. I enjoy hearing things like I have done a good job, or I have made someone feel happy. For people pleasers, these kind of words of affirmation are the proverbial cherry on the cake! We simply need to get better at hearing ourselves say those words to our self.

Reflection Point:
Find out what your love language is and commit to showing yourself what you need.

A General Note on Rejection

Rejection can feel painful, so much so that we do anything we can to avoid it (which is the perfect bait for your people pleaser). Nobody wants to feel rejected; we don't need further proof of how 'not enough' we are. However, avoiding the pain by trying to outsmart rejection at every turn is exhausting and wastes your immeasurable skills and energy.

One survival strategy that people pleasers adopt is to make themselves majorly amenable. Another is to become indispensable. Outrunning rejection becomes a skill, but when you do experience rejection as a people pleaser, it floors you. I was devastated when a person I had dated a few times ghosted me. 'What could I have done differently?' 'What was wrong with me?' Repeatedly, I replayed various scenarios and endless reasons for the rejection in my mind. All of the blame landed on me. Probably, he didn't want the hassle of texting to say he wasn't interested. However, I made it all about me. *I'd* done something wrong. *I* wasn't good enough. The rejection cut deep; it felt so personal.

Fast forward to last year and I discovered that quite a few women who had been early members of a group I ran had unfriended me on Facebook. This time, I didn't take the rejection personally. I knew that my being more vocal about social issues such as racism wasn't landing with some people; it wasn't the message they were ready (or wanting) to hear. And that's okay. I remained curious but wasn't emotionally attached to their rejection of me; I knew it was as much a part of their journey as it was mine. I no longer needed their validation – a huge win for any people pleaser! The difference came from releasing my need to please on a daily basis. Little by little, the validation I now have for myself - being my own best friend and supporting me - means my outlook has shifted. Now, I'm not going to pretend that if I was majorly rejected now that it wouldn't hurt. I'm human. I'm sensitive. And, like you, I feel *everything*. The difference now is that I harness my sensitivity and emotional awareness as a gift rather than allowing myself to feel burdened by them.

11
Female Misogynists

The New Wave of feminism post #metoo has heralded a new space or (let us be honest) a promise of a new space for women to take residency. However, patriarchy, people-pleasing, structural racism, and internalised misogyny are still so prolific due to unconscious bias that it is difficult to own these spaces fully.

I won't go into structural racism. I'm not an expert on intersectional feminism and structural racism, and for the study of this, I would urge you to seek out BIPOC teachers (see the resources section on page 165 for the educators I have learned from). Racism is deeply entrenched, and white people have a responsibility to educate ourselves and examine our own biases. I do, however, want to take a moment to discuss women who display misogynistic tendencies, thoughts and behaviours. These perpetuate people-pleasing. When women do not feel supported by other women - through negative experiences or lack of women around them - the beliefs they have grown up with are internalised into misogyny alongside the misogynistic notions from history and popular culture. A lot of misogyny is internalised as shame which we then project onto other women (and our daughters), continuing the misogynistic cycle.

We all have internalised misogyny within us, even if we think we do not. Just take a moment to pause and reflect on your attitude towards working mums or stay-at-home mums, for example. Perhaps you judge women who choose not to have children and/or women who have 'more than their fair share'. Do you claim to be a feminist yet hold prejudice towards trans women?

How do you view promiscuous women versus promiscuous men? Maybe you have a lot of negative thoughts around scantily clad women, or even women wearing hijabs and covering their body from head-to-toe.

How do you feel about women and their use of expletive language? I can guarantee that you have a lot of negative thoughts and opinions around women compared with men, especially in terms of mothering, appearance and sexuality, and this is before we add intersections such as class, gender identity and race. You may not have been aware of your biases until I posed the questions just now. Viewing women as anything other than equal to men is a symptom of internalised misogyny.

Internalised misogyny also plays out in the measure of our worth and how we show up and express our self in the world. As a people-pleaser, on some level, you do not believe you, as a woman, are worthy of X simply because you are a woman. This is not another stick to beat yourself up with but an opportunity to reflect. Like any prejudice or bias, most of this lies in our unconscious mind. When I think back to times that I've people pleased, I believed (consciously) that I wasn't worthy of X, and (unconsciously) that I was not worthy of X *because* I was a woman.

Note: this isn't about being anti-man or saying that 'all men are arseholes'. When we consider the patriarchy, for example, we are talking about a system that favours and gives societal privileges to men *because of* their gender. When we're talking about misogyny, we're talking about an imbalance of power. Due to historical and societal attitudes and beliefs about women (how they 'should' be and how they 'should' behave), and taking into account the drama triangle as discussed in chapter 8, men assume the dynamic of the 'perpetrator' while women become the 'victim'. As women, we have internalised this dynamic and the associated beliefs meaning that we, too, view women as 'less than' (mostly unconsciously), projecting our own insecurities onto other women while being blind to the dynamics at play.

Reflection Point:

How has internalised misogyny affected your beliefs about women being acceptable or not?

Section 3

People Pleasing ... In Work

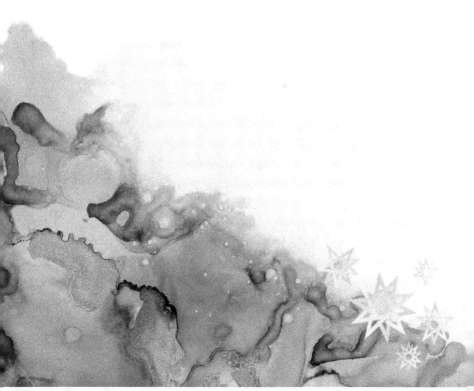

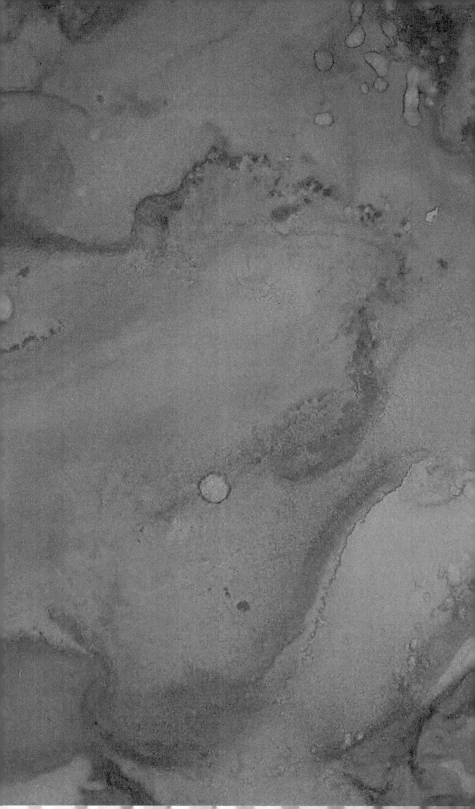

In this section, we are going to examine how the workplace culture can be a fertile ground for people pleasing. From my research into this topic it became apparent very quickly that, if you identify as a women, you are more likely to people please at work. Of course, there are plenty of women who do not people please. Likewise, men aren't immune from people pleasing at work. However, at the risk of generalising, it appears to be more of an issue for those who identify as female.

We are going to look at what it means to be nice versus assertive in your workplace, and what happens when you are leading a team as a people pleaser. It appears that some of the discrepancies between men and women at work could be down to people pleasing expectations. Get ready to challenge how you are being at work, and challenge the workplace culture that rewards people pleasing.

12
The Post-Metoo Workplace

Metoo, the call for the gender pay gap to be cut, increased awareness of companies' hiring practices, and workplace culture call-outs have brought an increased accountability to what is happening in our work environments. This increased accountability and attention means the discrepancies between women and men in the workplace have become glaringly obvious. So, why is there an expectation of you to please people at work?

Sarah says: 'At work, I push myself and take on extra responsibilities because there is an expectation I will say yes. Years of feeling the pressure to be that person who goes out of their way to help can be emotionally exhausting. Other people will argue about certain things while I will just get on with them, whether I agree or not – I don't want to cause a fuss.'

Ah, the 'I don't want to cause a fuss' scenario. We knew it was coming, right? In reality, few of us want to cause a fuss at work. But why does saying no or not being the one who volunteers for everything have to mean you are causing a fuss? Is this down to feeling we have to prove ourselves in order to be accepted at work? I want you to take a moment to consider the unseen labour you do at work. Consider the energy and effort you put in to come across as 'nice' and amenable. Do you spend time correcting the tone and language in your emails so that you don't come across as too 'bossy' or assertive? How about the conversations you rehearse in your head to appease the person who causes you stress at work? Perhaps you can see some of you in what Sarah has shared above – feeling emotionally exhausted and wanting to get through your day without 'causing a fuss'.

I'm not saying you should walk into work tomorrow, tell everyone to fuck off, and sit eating crisps while surfing the internet all day – that is a sure way to get fired! There is, of course, workplace etiquette. You have your specific responsibilities and understand your contractual obligations and code of conduct. Besides, you likely enjoy interacting with your colleagues (some of them anyway), and want to keep your job! What I am suggesting is that you look at how much energy and effort you're expending to people please. There are other more constructive ways to invest your talents, energy and focus into your personal and professional development, and enjoyment.

A quick word on authenticity and 'being authentic'. What I'm about to share can be applied to any of the topics we've covered in this book so far but it feels pertinent to share it in this chapter. Authenticity is a word that gets banded around a lot, particularly when we're talking about personal and professional development. 'Just be yourself.' 'Just do you.' 'Be more you.' Sound familiar?

Before I go on, I want to acknowledge that for some people, showing up whole-heartedly as their true self isn't safe. Some cultures are still unaccepting of homosexuality, for example, while a woman may adopt more 'masculine' traits to feel safer in a heavily male-dominated environment. In these situations it's understandable why some people would hide parts of themselves and would more consciously choose to be amenable to others.

Being authentic is not just about expressing who you are without the need to hide behind a mask, or creating a more socially acceptable alter-ego. It's certainly not about being rude and brash and telling everyone what you really think about them under the guise of being 'authentic'. But it is about relating more authentically to others in the way that we connect and communicate.

In the workplace, there is often a culture of pushing through, working harder and longer, and wearing 'busy' as a badge of honour – perfect ammo for people pleasing! There is always a boss, team member, or demanding client to be placated. Repeatedly working above and beyond on projects, consistently appeasing difficult team members, or accommodating virtually impossible requests because they are an important client – this culture thrives on compete and compare.

In an ideal world, we would all be supported to be our authentic selves at work. People would get their job based on merit, and teams would thrive based on genuine connection and effective communication.

There needs to be some pretty seismic attitude changes to allow for people pleasing to stop at work. You can contribute to change through your actions and beliefs, and improve how much you appreciate yourself at work instead of seeking validation from others.

Marike says: 'From my own experience as a woman in science, the times when I am being assertive or taking on a leadership position, people (almost always men) in my professional and personal circles have commented on how I'm not being nice enough, not feminine, not ladylike, not 'my sweet self' etc. '

Michelle adds: 'I've had times when my hard work and extra hours have gone unnoticed, and not being vocal about how busy I am has impacted my ranking in the bonus pool. I've waited for someone else to leave the office first (even if it meant missing my train and being late home), and felt guilty for taking a day off to look after my sick child. But, most notably, are the times when I've stood up for what's right. When I've spoken truth to power. I've been labelled a trouble maker many times; it seems most of my jobs have preferred the nice, quiet and amenable version of me.'

This is what you are going to come up against – other people wanting you to be nice at work because it benefits them and upholds their status quo. It makes their life easier. Having compliant, easy going yes people in your team, or as your employees, means less hassle. Are you ready to shake the foundations by not being nice?

Reflection Point:
Take a moment to reflect on what will change for you if you dropped the façade of niceness.

Remember: being nice isn't the same as being kind, and the autonym of nice isn't 'bitch' (though, let's face it, if you're not amenable as a woman then you may be labelled such. Thank you, misogyny!).

Let's say Marike has discovered a new piece of research which contradicts the work of a member of her team. They have a conversation and the other person, let's call them Jo, is hoping that Marike won't bring it up at their next team discussion. Jo, who is dismissive of the research, reminds Marike how much work would be created by introducing it. Marike has two options:

a) To be nice and not bring up this piece of research. She is super aware of Jo's attitude and can see how this could cause conflict between them at work. She also doesn't want to 'cause a fuss'.

b) To stick to what is right for her and to introduce this new piece of research.

If you were in the same predicament, which option would you choose?

The workplace is filled with nice Marikes and Michelles and, let's face it, we like them – they make life easy. But here's some recent statistics for where we are at with women in the workplace in the UK. As of April 2019, there are *no* sectors in the UK where women are paid the same as men, even when they're doing **exactly the same job**. None. Baffling that this is the 21st century and this is the working landscape. (Source, *Financial Times*.)

I must mention that for Black women and women of colour this gap is even larger. In the UK, women from minoritised groups don't even know how big a pay gap they may be experiencing as companies only break it down by male and female. The Fawcett Society are currently researching the issues surrounding Black women and women of colour in the workplace. Alongside the pay gap, there are multiple other issues that Black women and women of colour face, as well as members of the LGQBTIA community – so many more issues that could contribute to the need to people please.

I'm not saying that ditching your people pleasing will change these issues. Deep reform and seismic attitude changes are needed. Some things *are* changing, of course. We have progressed beyond only being employed as secretaries in the workplace, or being expected to resign once married, as was still the case for many companies in the 70s. There is still a long way to go, however. It stands to reason that if you are a white woman reading this and you do the work on people pleasing in the workplace, you can also be doing the work to support women of colour in your workplace too. What support can you offer? How can you be an ally? Please check out the resources section on page 165 for my suggestions on BIPOC educators who can support you with this.

What I am suggesting though is that, alongside workplace reform and deeper accountability, these big attitude changes need to be supported by women (in particular) quitting people pleasing at work. If you are feeling this, then you need to work on WHY you are people pleasing at work, and the associations of being nice versus being assertive. Being your wellbeing warrior is crucial when you are taking action to ditching your people pleaser. You need a daily practice which incorporates your Essential Me Time Maintenance, and a commitment to fierce love for yourself.

Let's go back to Marike. Being 'nice', Marike didn't put forward the new piece of research. What is the consequence of that? This new piece of research could be uncovered by another researcher who then gets the credit. She might stall in her career. She may feel disempowered, less than, inauthentic, and lacking in integrity. This will all have a knock-on effect on Marike's confidence. She will begin to doubt herself and hold herself back. She could get resentful, and so much negativity could breed from here.

How about 'assertive' Marike? She puts forward the piece of new research. She has some snarky behaviour to deal with from her team. Perhaps she gets the cold shoulder for a while. Not great BUT what could happen from here? She gets given a new project to work on, or another organisation sees her work and hires her. Perhaps nothing spectacular happens but instead she has ownership over her views, trusts her judgement, and feels more confident. Maybe next time Jo won't presume she will be nice and will treat her with more equality and respect. What Jo does or doesn't do isn't important. What Marike does and how she feels as a result of not people pleasing is what counts. From here on in, what you do and how you feel as a result of not people pleasing is what matters.

We cannot discount the ripple effect as well. Let's say a few other women in Marike's team sees what she has done. They know Jo, too. OK, it's fair to assume there may be some bitchiness. But a few women would look at Marike and think, 'Hell yes. She has stood in her power. Maybe I could do that too.'

So perhaps, instead of volunteering to organise the staff Christmas do, and being the one doing the dishes or the one who laughs everything off, you make some decisions to stand more in your power at work. You can still be a kind, considerate and supportive member at work without disempowering yourself. Now, I am not saying this will be easy. It won't. And there might be some women who have deep internal misogyny (see chapter 11) who will bitch about you behind your back (or passive-aggressively within earshot). Attitudes don't change overnight.

Let's look at another scenario – people pleasing because of bitchy women at work. Yes, the workplace is, sadly, still a breeding ground for playground-style bitchiness.

Let me introduce you to Ayesha. She is good at everything but never likes to show anyone else up. Ayesha is funny, bright, multi-talented, and someone who champions other women. She is also a people pleaser. She is effortlessly popular but doesn't believe in herself so is continuously self-deprecating, i.e. *I'll put myself down in a more funny and sharp way than you could.* She's damn good at putting herself down and she's funny so people laugh with her. People also pick up consciously, or unconsciously, on how she comes across. 'Pushover.' 'Too nice.' 'She'll never say no.' Can you recognise any of this in you or in your relationships? And maybe, just maybe, you recognise these judgments that you, yourself, have made about other women. Oooh … that's a radical (and uncomfortable) sprinkle of self-awareness, right there!

Ayesha manages a team of women in a charitable organisation and she has recently been promoted. She is starting to notice that a few of her team are not contributing: their work is lacklustre, their attitude is poor, and they are having a negative impact on their team performance and morale. She isn't feeling confident about how to approach this – she doesn't want her team to dislike her.

Reflection Point:
Let's take a moment here. This is your cue to stop and think how many times at work you've been in situations where you have been worried about your team mates disliking you. And yes, I am looking at YOU. How much energy have you exhausted on this?

Newly promoted, Ayesha wants to take time to get to know her team and how best to manage them. She conducts considerate one-to-ones where she coaches each of them, setting up action plans and review dates. This works with a couple of them; it turns out they have been previously mismanaged and micro managed. The consideration and time Ayesha spends with them really pays off. However, with Hayley, it doesn't. She does the bare minimum and is now talking to other teams about how crap a manager Ayesha is.

Ayesha feels like she's back at square one – she consumes so much energy trying to find a way to deal with this. She talks over the situation with her friends, going around in circles and not coming up with any solution that doesn't involve Hayley not liking her. Well, she could do nothing, right? She could just carry on trying to appease Hayley – but at what cost?

- Her team's performance suffers

- Their projects could struggle to come together

- Ayesha has a ton more work and stress

Most importantly, Ayesha's confidence and belief in herself will weaken and, let's be really honest here, Hayley isn't going to like or respect her more. Instead, she'll continue treating Ayesha with contempt, and this will rub off on other team members and have long-term detrimental effects. Ayesha needs to do something radical for *her*. She needs to not be nice.

Ayesha knows something needs to change. She goes through the 7-Step Exploration, uses the resources to support her in remembering who she wants to be at work and, most importantly, makes a choice to not people please. She listens to her intuition which is telling her to have an official structured and brave conversation with Hayley at work. Ayesha invites Hayley to be honest too, but sets a tone of total professionalism. She decides that Hayley doesn't have to like her but Ayesha does want to be treated with respect. She does it her way, compassionately and with boundaries.

You are going to face some resistance and potentially some bitchiness at work. The choice lies with you. Do you want to people please to try and make everyone like you or, and this is a total cliché, be true to you and be guided by your values of compassion and courage? Ultimately, you have no control over other people's opinions and feelings. Trying to control them is a form of manipulation coming from a place of fear.

If you are guided by your personal values, then other people may not like you – but *you* will like you. At the end of the day, as you're the one who has to spend time with yourself every day, your own self-respect is much more important.

And I must inform you that Ayesha *did* deal with Hayley in a compassionate way, and Hayley decided to leave the team. Now Ayesha's team is a buzzing, supportive and successful team who have won awards in their sector. Most crucially, Ayesha feels she appreciates and respects herself at work, and doesn't feel the need to please.

Reflection Point:

Reflect on how you've enabled people pleasing behaviour and how past or current situations at work have been created through your need to be liked, your need for approval, and your fear of being seen in a certain way.

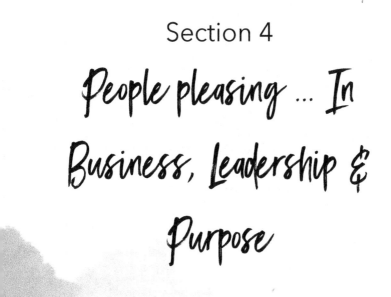

Section 4

People pleasing ... In Business, Leadership & Purpose

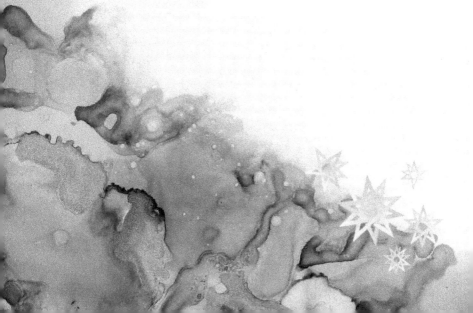

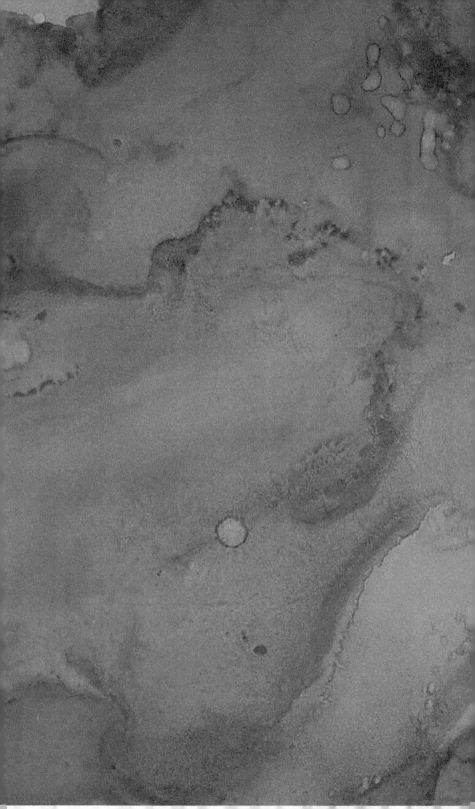

Whether you have a business, consider yourself a leader, or know what your purpose is (or not), this section is for you. If you have a business right now, and want it to be successful, you need to get up close and personal with your people pleaser – otherwise, she will block your path and put a glass-ceiling on your success! Your business is an extension of you, your values, and the time and energy you pour into it. If you're people pleasing in your business, you are stunting your growth.

If you don't currently have your own business but plan to in the future, the principles I share in this section will help prevent people pleasing issues early on, and make starting your business a bit less painful.

Being a leader in these times calls for complete authenticity and to show up fully. Neither of these happen when your people pleaser is running the show. Being a leader looks and feels very different to different people in different situations, whether that be leading as the parent you want to be, as the friend you want to be, or through championing a project you want to start up. People pleasing can affect all forms of leadership and make everything much more challenging.

People pleasing can stop the right clients/audience/contacts from connecting with you. When you let go of being nice and diluting your message to make it more palatable, or stop weakening your boundaries around the terms of your business, for example, potential clients will feel your authentic energy and everything will click into place.

We close this section (and book) with your purpose – the holy grail of what we spend so much time as business owners and leaders searching for. What your work, leadership, and business represents is an external manifestation of your purpose. Blocking this by people pleasing is a waste of your innate gifts, and a real disservice to you and the world.

In this section, I'm going to share personal experiences of being an entrepreneur for 10 years, having had a 6-figure business and won multiple awards. While that sounds good (and I'm proud of my achievements), I'm most proud of the times I've conducted business *my* way, when I've lead with courage and compassion, and when I've fully embodied my purpose. I want to share insights and techniques to support you with ditching people pleasing in your business so that you, too, can connect to your purpose, and use your superpowers (gifts) to be an effective leader, not just in business, but in all areas of your life.

13

The Five Superpowers

It feels great to finish this book talking about the five Sensitive Superpowers. You have many, of course, but I want to highlight the main five that I use in my own work, and with my community. They each play a significant part in how you love, live, work, lead and connect. I'm going to take you through each Superpower so that you can get a sense of how, by ditching your people pleaser, you can use them to their fullest capacity as you blaze the trail in your business (and life).

I talk about Purpose, Platform and Privilege in my work. What I mean by these terms are as follows:

Purpose: What you have come on this earth to do and

experience. If, right now, you're not sure what that is, trust that your journey to letting go of your people pleaser will take you closer; all will unfold.

Platform: The small or large platform you have - whether that be social media and/or friends, colleagues, clients and family - where you can influence by sharing your thoughts and ideas.

Privilege: I refer to my privilege as my white skin privilege - the societal advantages that I am afforded because I am white – and use it to amplify marginalised voices to support the movement for social justice.

People pleasing can affect each of these three things and the impact we desire to make. Leadership requires that we use our platforms and privilege for the greater good and step fully into our purpose – very hard when your people pleaser is running the show!

By default of not people pleasing, you are being a leader in your work (and life). Not conforming to social or family norms or pressure means that you are forging a new path. Sometimes you have role models; sometimes you don't. Creating that new path and walking it calls for you to connect with five of your Sensitive Superpowers. These superpowers will serve and support you –

so long as you commit to ditching the need to please.

Courage

What this superpower means for a recovering people pleaser:

The courage to listen to what is important to you. The courage to not do what someone else wants you to do. The courage to say no.

The challenge for you to work on:

Learning how to say no.

When I first started off in self-employment as a contractor, I felt the need to say yes to all clients, to all the demands, and to make sure everyone was happy. The idea of saying no, of turning a client away, or of not taking the first rate I was offered was scary. What if the work dried up? What if no money came in? I ended up working all-consuming hours (never able to switch off), was available 24/7 (hello, lack of boundaries), and was under charging. Most importantly, I undervalued the work I was doing. It was incredibly exhausting.

In my first business, t.e.a.m, my business partner and I were so new to the game. We had zero business experience and no money behind us. We were literally building our business on enthusiasm alone, which we both had in abundance. We set up our training and workshops and then worked backwards, building the business around those offerings. One manager, who we had worked for before, wanted to invest in our training but kept haggling on the price. She ended up paying the least for our services *and* was the most difficult and demanding of all our clients. We very quickly learned to firm up our boundaries!

It was lucky that I learned this lesson so early on in my business. I found that saying no to clients that did not fit or who tried to cut my prices freed up time, energy and availability for clients who were a much better fit. It meant being courageous enough to say no.

We didn't do much more training with that particular manager, but we did have the space to be able to work with other managers who were happy to pay our rates and were a joy to work with.

Customer service and satisfaction in whatever your business or projects provide is paramount – but does people pleasing equal good results? In a nutshell, no. Energy is important. Even if we can't articulate 'that' feeling, we get a sense of something being 'off' in our gut. Sometimes the vibe simply isn't right. If we are feeling this, yet still find ourselves saying yes to something that ought to be a hard no, then we need to check in with our people pleaser.

Being courageous enough to say no to people is fundamental to your success in business; to showing up as the leader you want to be, and to get closer to your purpose.

Reflection Point:

What does courage feel like for you? How is people pleasing stopping you from fully accessing it?

Empathy

What this superpower means for a recovering people pleaser:

To fully feel and process your own energy and emotions for clarity and confidence. It is vital that you understand what energy is yours, and what isn't.

Challenge for you to work on:

How to maintain strong and healthy boundaries.

Having empathy is such a gift to me in my business and

leadership, and is a huge part of my purpose.

However, it took me several years to get to this point. Throughout my business, I've been a coach in various guises. For some time, I had weak boundaries within my coaching sessions, allowing people to off load everything onto me. So, I would get exhausted or overwhelmed. An example is when I used to lead an in person membership group for female entrepreneurs. I would lead a workshop for the morning with a tea break half way through. For the first six months, I'd never have a break, as that tea break would end up with someone off-loading onto me. I'd run to the toilet moments before the second half started and feel my energy lagging. I wanted to please everyone and be available for them to chat with me but it was exhausting. I knew something had to shift. In this instance, I set myself a boundary: I'd finish the first half, leave the space, and return to start the second half. I stuck with it. It felt so much better for my energy and the overall energy of the workshop. Consider it this way – if you want to help and support people, you can only do that if you help and support yourself.

For you that might look like:

- Taking breaks when you are working

- Doing your practice before you start work

- Knowing the warning signs of overwhelm and course correcting accordingly

- Stating your boundaries - out loud, in writing, on social media, in client contracts, on your website - and following through with them

- If you say something isn't acceptable, being prepared to stand by it

Empathy without kindness to yourself has a limit, or becomes conditional upon others in your work. Empathy when you have worked on your people pleaser means you are open and clear *because* you have boundaries. This is where you step up as a leader and become the conduit for change.

Reflection Point:
How could your empathy support you in your business/as a leader/in your purpose? Where do you need to create boundaries to detach from people pleasing?

Compassion in Action

What this superpower means for a recovering people pleaser:

It means embodying your values and expressing them without fear of what someone might think. It means being prepared to be judged and to be visible. Your people pleaser will try and stop you from being hurt this way, but your embodiment and devotion means more than whether some people like you or not.

Challenge for you to work on:

Taking the action regardless of what others think because you know it is in alignment with you.

I feel it is crucial to talk about the importance of this superpower as a leader. Sensitive leadership means listening, learning, educating yourself, and course correcting. It means knowing that, however good your intention, sometimes the impact will not turn out so well. Compassion in action means being ready to apologise. There is a big difference between playing to the crowd (people pleasing) and listening to understand what you need to do differently.

Compassion without action is lip service. Within your business, leadership, and connecting with your purpose, compassion in action means you are engaging in real life.

Only you can determine your visibility within any area of your life. If you are invested in your work - whether that be a side hustle, your own business, or a project - shrinking to be more palatable or less threatening to others will do you and your business a huge disservice. You need to feel your full being in all of your work and people need to see and feel you. 'Don't get too big for your boots,' , 'Who does she think she is,' etc. are all constraints designed to keep you small and towing the line.

Take a moment now to absorb these words: you must get comfortable with the idea that you are going to piss someone off, that your work isn't for everyone, and that you will probably shine a bit too bright for some people.

With the arrival of social media, society has become a lot more transparent in many ways, not necessarily in terms of truth, but in how visible we all are. Very little is off limits nowadays, from what people are eating for breakfast, to their favourite Netflix shows, to the passive-aggressive arguments they're having. With your work, you will be on social media in some way and with that comes judgement. You may have heard it said that people are too busy thinking about themselves and their own lives to be judging you. It's not true. People judge. They will judge whatever you say or do, or don't say or do. You'll be judged for being vocal. You'll be judged for your silence. Make no mistake – you *will* be judged. Therefore, it saves a lot of time and heartache for you to do your work the way *you* want to and, as many a popular song would say, let the haters hate! You cannot please everyone, and neither is it your job to, so why not stick to pleasing yourself with your work. Mistakes are part of having your own business (and indeed part of being alive), and if your fear of being judged stems from perfectionism, you have it in you to let that go.

I've had people tell me they judged me – I've spoken in front of large audiences, been the guest blogger in other spaces, and written about my experiences of being abused. None of these experiences felt comfortable, but they are not meant to. Sometimes, I've felt incredibly nervous but the desire to fully expand and be present in my work has been much bigger than the worry of other people judging me.

This superpower has to come from a place of deep compassion for yourself and others which is cultivated through your imperfect practice.

Reflection Point:

Where is your need to please people preventing you from using your voice/platform/privilege? What difference could you make if you weren't worried about what other people thought?

Creativity

What this superpower means for a recovering people pleaser:

The ability to understand what your creativity looks and feels like. To express yourself creatively.

Challenge for you to work on:

Discover what creativity means for you and go with it without waiting for validation.

When you are people pleasing, you are disconnected with your Higher Self. You are also disconnected with your creativity. You might be relying on others to give you ideas, or not moving forward until your idea has been validated with the approval of others.

I've had the pleasure of working with a range of women who have had amazing projects/businesses/ideas. A significant proportion struggled with others' perceptions of who they 'should' be in their business, how much they 'should' charge for projects, and how confident or not they 'should' be. Success – whatever that means, feels or looks like to you - can only be accessed through your creative expression.

Writing a book about people pleasing as a recovering people pleaser has been a brilliant exploration of what creative expression really means to me. I want this book to be valuable to you. I also don't want to write what I am 'expected' to write, or to conform to what a traditional self-help book might look like. I've followed my intuitive guidance when I feel something needs to be said. I've shared from my heart and expressed myself in the way that is my truth right now. This kind of creativity connects and creates in a way that is much more powerful than conforming to whatever self-help standard is currently popular. How I express myself in six months, one year, and five years from now will be different. Right now, it matters to me that I am authentic in my creative expression in this moment. This has been made possible because I'm no longer concerned about what others think.

Reflection Point:

Where are you giving your creative power away by waiting for validation for your ideas? How could being connected to your creative expression change things for you in your business/as a leader/through your purpose?

Intuition

What this superpower means for a recovering people pleaser:

Being guided by your intuition, not from your ego, allowing you to make great business decisions. You listen to your inner voice, not the critics.

Your challenge to work on:

Tuning out the external noise so you can hear your intuition.

I vividly remember a conversation with my mum. I was on a train and had called her. It was at the height of t.e.a.m's success and I was excited to let Mum know about the awards we were nominated for. She listened to me, congratulated me, and then said, 'But you don't want to get too successful now.' I'll let that sink in for a moment. I actually cannot remember what I said in response but the memory stayed with me. It surfaced again not that long ago when I was working on some beliefs I had around money and success. There were some limitations I had faced, and the idea of not getting 'too big for your boots' is one that I'd heard so many times when I was young. These kinds of stories disconnect you from your intuition.

I realised that people pleasing isn't just about my experience, but also about modelling a strong empowered presence for my child and breaking generations of playing small, trying to meet expectations, and not listening to intuitive guidance. My mum had a strong creative and entrepreneurial streak, my grandma too – it was probably called 'resourceful' in her generation. However, it was only allowed to a certain point. They were both highly intuitive but never fully trusted their intuition. My grandma had amazing psychic gifts but didn't trust in herself enough to use them. My mum had amazing healing abilities but would never allow herself to fully heal in order to completely embody those abilities. I'm here breaking all the cycles. I didn't follow any rulebook to start my own business, and I didn't wait for anyone's permission to be a mamma and an entrepreneur. I'm owning my psychic gifts and my healing abilities. However, it took constant awareness of those inherently ingrained generational stories to lift my limitations. It took dedication to my intuition.

Reflection Point:
How much are you guided by ego to make decisions? What are you going to start/stop doing so that you can connect with your intuition regularly?

Have you fallen into the hole of trying to please others before yourself in your business or as a leader? Perhaps it has been because of fear of judgement, or playing small to fit an expectation someone else has of you? It's time to blast through these toxic stories and step fully into the possibility and potential of your work.

Our voices can be heard in a completely new way. What a privilege it is to be able to share, help to inform, and signpost for the greatest good! As leaders, we can build deeper connections, foster empathy, and amplify what isn't being heard.

We have been blessed to be born into these somewhat challenging times with access to support and connection like no other. The internet has made the world and business more accessible, connecting us to resources, opportunities, people, and infinite possibilities that our mothers and grandmothers didn't have. Let us not blow this opportunity through people pleasing. What a waste of your gifts that would be.

There is no time to waste. Your people and the world need you. They need you fully in your power, remembering who you are – away from people pleasing. The ways you can help, the ideas that you have, the causes that need your support, the voices you need to amplify, and your God given purpose all demand that you let go of the need to please and be 'nice', and fully embody your gifts.

A Note on Purpose

If you don't feel like you know what your purpose is, you're not alone. We can become so fixated (and frustrated) on finding our purpose but if you don't yet know what it is, that's OK. Honestly. I can assure you that you're on the right path, right now.

Some people may say, 'My purpose is to experience joy,' while others are looking for nirvana. For some, it's about being at One; for others, it's feeling fulfilled. As our ego plays such a huge part in our experience of life, my genuine number one tip for connecting with your purpose is to make connecting with the present moment a top priority *even if* the present moment feels particularly uncomfortable and challenging. It could be considered that we have an inner and an outer purpose – your inner purpose related to connection to your Highest Self/Source, and your outer to your contribution with your gifts in the world.

Connecting with your superpowers will bring you closer to your inner *and* outer purpose. Each of the superpowers I have shared in this section help to connect you in a deep way. Here's how:

Courage: to access your courage, build it like a muscle and practice it means you are coming closer and closer to your purpose. You can't practice courage and not be allowing space for your purpose to come through.

Empathy: as a sensitive, your empathy is innate. When you are connected to your empathy in an empowered way (with boundaries and deep awareness), you pave the way for your purpose to come through you.

Compassion in Action: every time you take action based on an issue that is important to you, e.g. something that you cannot stay silent on, you are moving into your purpose. Each time you hear something and it moves you, and you feel called to speak up about it, you are moving into your purpose.

Creativity: your creativity is part of your Soul's expression, however that looks for you. Each time you tap into your creativity, you are tapping into your Soul's expression and inviting your purpose to move in and out of you.

Intuition: this is your innate knowing and is inextricably linked with your purpose. Your Soul's whispers come through your intuition and bring you together with your purpose. Stay close to your intuition – your purpose is there.

Your purpose may change at different stages of your life, and that's also OK. The more you grow and evolve, so too will your purpose. Right now, you could say that your purpose is to ditch the need to please. The more you continue to people please, the more you block your connection to Self and therefore your purpose. Making the decision (again and again) to blaze your own trail and fully committing to being all of you (and never again losing yourself to people pleasing) is purpose in itself.

Section 5

The 7-Step Exploration

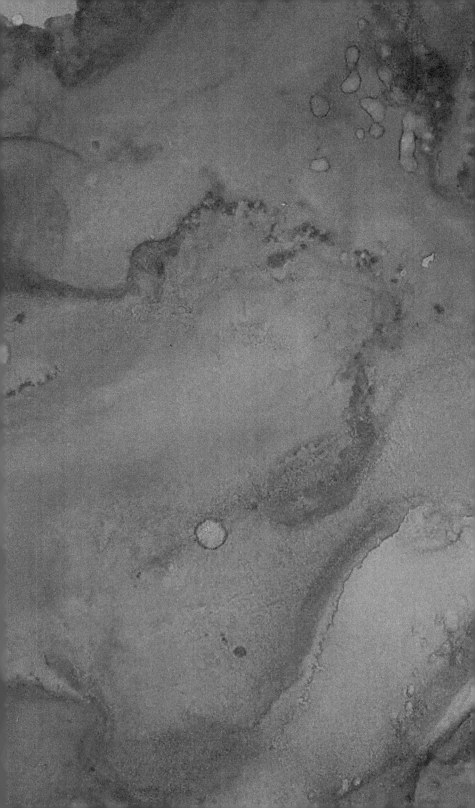

I am delighted you are making the decision to ditch your people pleaser. Please work through this exploration step by step. Make it applicable and relevant for you. Take your time, breathe deep, move your body, and connect with your Self before you start each step. I would recommend meditating (or doing something to drop into a meditative state) beforehand, so that you can access your intuition and write free-flow. You may also wish to listen to my **Yoga Nidra MP3** to evoke the relaxation response (access it here: www.soulconfidence.co.uk/ditch-the-people-pleaser-resources).

Remember: this is not a cookie cutter process. This is an exploration for you to meet you where you are at and support yourself on your journey to ditch your people pleaser.

A pdf of the full 7-step process can be downloaded here: www.soulconfidence.co.uk/ditch-the-people-pleaser-resources

Step 1:
Awareness & the Origin Stories

Where does your people pleaser show up?

_____

_____

_____

_____

_____

In what areas of your life does your people pleaser show up?

_____

_____

_____

_____

_____

Why do they appear there?

_____

_____

_____

_____

_____

_____

_____

Are there specific times or circumstances that they come up?

_____

_____

_____

_____

_____

_____

_____

Can you reflect on where your people pleaser first appeared?

_____

_____

_____

_____

_____

_____

_____

What is the story your people pleaser is telling you?

_____

_____

_____

_____

_____

_____

_____

Step 2:
Surrender & Letting Go

Instead of fighting your people pleaser or trying to pretend they are not there, surrender to the fact that your people pleaser has been showing up for a reason. You can let go of them being 'in charge' by accepting that they are formed from your experiences/fear and have functioned to protect you.

Spend some time acknowledging this, and write out your reflections around being a people pleaser and the role that they have been playing in your life, choices and behaviour to date.

Step 3:
Fierce Love

Treat yourself as your own best friend with loving kindness. Fierce love means you recognise and accept all of who you are and you show up 100 % for your life, gifts, purpose and Higher Self.

Write out your Fierce Love commitment to yourself.

'I am committed to showing up with fierce love to myself by ...'

_____

_____

_____

_____

_____

_____

_____

_____

Step 4:
Be Your Wellbeing Warrior

Being your wellbeing warrior is crucial to supporting yourself on your journey to ditching your people pleaser. You have to know what you need and when you need it to keep yourself filled up. Depletion and overwhelm will see you slipping back into the old patterns of people pleasing. In this step, get clear on what your Essential Me Time Maintenance (EMTM) looks like (this can incorporate your self-care, practice, and internal and external support systems. It also means your self-talk and boundaries).

Your Essential Me Time Maintenance needs to support you through your month and to work with your personal cycle and/or the moon cycle. For example, going to high impact aerobics classes during your period (if applicable) is not supporting you at that point of your personal cycle, but getting an early night and warm baths might. Equally, if you are connected to the Full Moon, you may find that Essential Me Time Maintenance for you at that time of the moon phase is drawing and creating, but doing an intensive breath workshop may not be for you at that point of the moon phase.

Write out what you want your Essential me time maintenance to incorporate. Include all the things that make you feel good, happy, healthy and supported. Write out what you can be doing daily/weekly/monthly. Also, get clear on what you want to do to support yourself with your personal cycle (if applicable) and/or the moon cycle.

_____

_____

_____

_____

_____

_____

_____

_____

_____

_____

_____

_____

_____

When are you going to schedule your EMTM, and how will you stay committed to being your wellbeing warrior?

_____

_____

_____

_____

_____

_____

_____

_____

_____

_____

_____

_____

_____

_____

_____

Make notes here, and then take aligned action. Don't just think it – set it up and do the things that make you feel good.

Remember to use the **Daily Presence Practice MP3** as part of your Essential Me Time Maintenance. You can access it here:

www.soulconfidence.co.uk/ditch-the-people-pleaser-resources

Step 5:
Choose Your Superpowers

You have a choice. You can choose to react from your people pleaser, OR you can choose to respond from being present to the now and deepen your superpowers.

For each of the five superpowers here, consider how letting go of people pleasing will impact your superpowers. Write out how you want to bring more of the five superpowers into all areas of your life.

Superpower 1: Empathy

_____

_____

_____

_____

_____

_____

_____

Superpower 2: Compassion in Action

_____

_____

_____

_____

_____

_____

Superpower 3: Courage

_____

_____

_____

_____

_____

_____

Superpower 4: Creativity

_____

_____

_____

_____

_____

_____

Superpower 5: Intuition

_____

_____

_____

_____

_____

_____

Step 6:
Gratitude

What has learning about your people pleaser given you? For example, what insights do you now have? Can you see how relationships could feel better and be more supportive? What difference has this awareness brought you in all areas of your life?

_____

_____

_____

_____

_____

_____

_____

_____

_____

_____

Where is the gold in this exploration for you?

_____

_____

_____

_____

_____

_____

_____

_____

_____

_____

_____

_____

_____

_____

_____

_____

_____

Step 7:
Commitment

Moving forward, what is your commitment to yourself over this work?

_____

_____

_____

_____

_____

How are you going to stay accountable to what you really want and need?

_____

_____

_____

_____

_____

How will you connect each day with the antidote – Put Yourself First?

_____

_____

_____

_____

_____

Create your commitment and decide on how you are going to connect every day with the antidote.

A Final Love Note From Kara

Let me finish with this love note to you.

My love, I'm truly proud of you for picking up this book and making a decision.

A decision to choose your own path away from the old stories of people pleasing.

A decision to feel all of your life, to connect with your purpose, and to show up for your people.

When you lose the need to please you are saying yes to everything that is inside you and available for you.

All of the time and energy you used up people pleasing can now be invested in you. People pleasing is a waste of your talents and skills: you have so much to offer that will be unlocked by lifting the weight of people pleasing, the ripple effect of which is immeasurable. Imagine the positive impact on the world, your relationships and, perhaps more importantly, the next generation. Your decision and actions are breaking the cycle of people pleasing; you are taking an active role in changing what it means to be acceptable and nice.

Society prefers you to be nice. Making a decision not to be is radical. Any time you're challenged with breaking the need to please, ask yourself: 'What do I care more about – living a life fully expressed, owning all of my superpowers, committing fully to the issues I care about and having real, honest and joyful relationships with the people I love? Or, what some people think (or might be thinking) about me?'

Remember, you quitting people pleasing isn't selfish. It doesn't mean you don't care anymore, or that you'll become hard and unfeeling. It's the opposite. You putting your needs first means there is more of you to go around. You can overflow with the good stuff and everyone (including you) feels the benefit. Your empathy and compassion will expand with those healthy boundaries and your superpowers will be heightened. When you look at things from this perspective, you can see that quitting people pleasing is, in fact, a selfless act.

You need to have the antidote on you at all times – Put Yourself First. This doesn't mean thinking, *I need to put myself first* then not doing it. It means taking aligned action consistently, especially (at first) when it feels difficult and painful. You've so many resources in this book to support you with this. Use them, not just once, but again and again and as much as you need.

You are clear now on why you are quitting people pleasing. Keep that close to you. You can see where your people pleasing originated from, and the stories and constructs that have created the idea of what 'nice' means. You can feel where people pleasing shows up and why you are letting it go. We've looked at our early years, some of the psychology behind people pleasing, and you now understand how different your relationships could feel when you aren't people pleasing.

Maybe, if you've been applying your learning as you've worked through this book, you'll already be feeling the difference. Perhaps you've made some different choices at work and realise that you can still be a kind colleague without doing everything for everyone. Maybe at home you've acknowledged some changes you want to make and taken action so you don't feel resentful or overwhelmed.

Those superpowers within you - courage, compassion in action, creativity, intuition and empathy - will continue to expand as you become more aligned with your Higher Self; as you remember the truth of who you are, away from the need to be accepted, to have approval, or to be validated. No more pushing things down or pretending – what a relief!

While I believe in taking one step at a time, I do need to stress the immediacy of you needing to break free from the people pleaser box. The world at the moment is changing rapidly, and you being here during this time is no coincidence. Do your work … but take your place in the world *now*.

Use the resources in this book to take your inner work to the next level. Refer back to the reflection questions when needed, and join our Facebook community - The Sensitive Superstars Movement - to share your journey.

One of the best things I ever did was quit people pleasing.

I know it will be one of the best things you will ever do, too.

Kara x

Resources

BIPOC Educators:

This is not an exhaustive list. I am sharing BIPOC educators and women of colour and Black women in the spiritual/Yoga communities who I have personally learned from.

Nova Reid: www.novareid.com

Kelsey Korero: www.thekorero.com

Susanna Barkataki: www.susannabarkataki.com

Faith Hunter: www.faithhunter.com

Dianne Bondy: www.diannebondyyoga.com

Michelle Johnson: www.michellecjohnson.com/about-1

All of the MP3s and other resources that I have mentioned in this book (including the downloadable 7-Step Exploration pdf) can be accessed here:

www.soulconfidence.co.uk / ditch-the-people-pleaser-resources

About the Author

Kara is a writer, Yoga teacher, intuitive coach, and multi award-winning entrepreneur.

Founder of the Sensitive Superstar Movement, she wants sensitives to flip the story of sensitivity being a weakness, and instead own it as their superpower.

Kara had a breakthrough on her 'journey' when she finally got it! She discovered that being sensitive can be amazing, and that her superpowers come from that sensitivity. She would LOVE to see a world where wealth is shared equally, the earth is respected and looked after, and everyone is given the same opportunities and freedom, regardless of race. She is committed to playing her part in creating that equitable world.

Kara likes being out under the stars at festivals, trying to keep plants alive, and eating vegan cakes.

Connect with Kara:

Website: www.soulconfidence.co.uk

Instagram: www.instagram.com/karavgrant

Facebook: www.facebook.com/sensitivesuperstars

Please join her free Facebook community The Sensitive Superstars Movement for support from other sensitive people who get what it means to be a people pleaser.

Acknowledgements

Firstly, to the brave people who emailed their stories and experiences to form the beating heart of this book.

To Scott, for his unwavering belief that I was going to get the book done, and his steadfast belief in me. For keeping all of our lives going around my writing.

To Michelle, the most patient and insightful editor I could have dreamed of.

To the writers on our retreats, whose passion inspired me.

To my community, whose enthusiasm on this topic kept me going.

To Arthur and Archie, for being the generation who will lead the change.

CPSIA information can be obtained
at www.ICGtesting.com
Printed in the USA
LVHW051420030621
689226LV00013B/595

9 781916 250499